☑ I live _____ miles f[...] [barcode: MW00469546]
miles from the geographic cerner of the United States.

☑ My favorite national park, monument, seashore, lakeshore, preserve, reserve, historic site, forest, or wildlife refuge
is / used to be _____

☑ My favorite government bureaucracy is the ____.
1) National Park Service 2) USDA Forest Service
3) U.S. Fish & Wildlife Service
4) Bureau of Land Management   OR
5) my local school district   6) other _____

☑ My favorite bear is the ____. 1) grizzly (brown) bear
2) black bear   3) polar bear
4) Smokey Bear   5) other _____

☑ Before I read this book, I ____.
1) had never heard of the jack-a-lope
2) believed the jack-a-lope was real
3) knew the jack-a-lope was a hoax   OR
4) I still believe the jack-a-lope is real.

☑ My favorite Ending is ____. 1) #1   2) #2

☑ I ____.   1) can't wait for the sequel
2) will contribute material or offer suggestions for a sequel
3) am writing my own sequel

☑ Where am I?

75 PAGES TO WALL DRUG

(IR)Rational Parks

An Offbeat Look at
Wilderness, Tourism, & America

David Blomstrom

(IR)Rationally Yours,

David Blomstrom

Library of Congress Catalog Number: 95-094662

International Standard Book Number (ISBN): 0-9646777-0-9

Grateful acknowledgment is made to the following for permission to reprint quotations, photographs, and illustrations from various sources:

Quotation Credits:
Pages 143-145 and 177 (along with the photograph on page 168) From THE BAT BOMB: WORLD WAR II'S OTHER SECRET WEAPON by Jack Couffer, Copyright © 1992. By permission of the author and the University of Texas Press.
Page 198: Article "Pearl Harbor: "When is the dolphin show?'" Reprinted with permission, *Chicago Sun-Times* © 1995.
Page 212: Article "Reversing the Tide: Washington Turns to Privatization to help reduce the budget deficit" Excerpt reprinted with permission, *U.S. News & World Report* © 1995.
Pages 111-113: Quotations attributed to Robert Kelleher, Jr. taken from article "Rematch at Little Big Horn" (*Montana Magazine*) © 1995, with permission of the author.

Illustration Credits:
Author front cover, 7, 27, 28, 40 (top), 101, 123, 128, 147 (Japanese Zeroes), 157, 191, 192, 201, 203, 208 Copyright © 1995; Flag Research Center: 40 (bottom), 122, Copyright ©; Ben Garrison: 10, 36-37, 39, 46, 48, 58, 64, 94-97, 103, 146-147, 176, 201, 203, 208, Copyright © 1995 (by author); Zoological Society of London 222

Photo Credits:
Author 164; *Bat Bomb* (University of Texas Press & Jack Couffer) 168; Bettmann Archive 93; Jeff Foott Photography 127; Robert Kelleher 114 and back cover; Montana State Highway Commission 12; National Park Service 12, 24, 104, 123 (Scotts Bluff National Monument), 128, 158, 181, 204, 205; North Dakota Game and Fish Department 100; St. Louis RCGA 20; South Dakota Department of Tourism 8, 92, 99 (top), 103; U.S. Army 6; Wall Drug 2, 99 (bottom), 102 (from book *Free Ice Water!*); Washington Convention and Visitors Bureau 24

DEDICATION

This book is dedicated to my parents — where would I be without them?

It is also dedicated to Park Rangers — including the late Edward Abbey, whose spirit lives on in this book; Bud Rice, who shared my first wilderness experience, during which we saw a wolverine; and the rangers who sent me the material without which this book could never have been written — whose love and respect for America's natural and cultural heritage, affection for visitors, and willingness to work for rock-bottom wages make them the federal bureaucracy's best bargain.

It is dedicated to teachers and parents — urban rangers of sorts who guide future generations of tourists through America's public education wilderness, especially to those teachers and parents — and future tourists — who know me as Mr. B.

Finally, it is dedicated to everyone who has ever been a tourist, especially to those who continue to ask questions no matter how silly they may seem. (If you ask a *really* silly one, let me know — perhaps I can use it in a sequel!)

Since almost every United States citizen has been a tourist, ranger, teacher, or parent at one time, I suppose I could simply dedicate it to Americans — but I already have.

Humanity's worst nightmare or just someone dynamiting Arizona petrified wood? It might be neither. Another nightmarish weapon was being tested in the Southwest alongside America's first atomic bombs. At the last minute, America threw its lot in with the atom. But for the whims of history, New Mexico's Carlsbad Caverns might be inhabited by terrorized people rather than bats. Learn the shocking details on page 143.

ACKNOWLEDGMENTS

I acknowledge the following for their invaluable assistance:

Gary Csillaghegyi, vexillographer and astronomer, for critiquing my manuscript and contributing a wealth of material related to flags and Petrified Forest National Park

Don Graydon, recreation book editor, for his critique and suggestions

Jay Lane and Judith Shane — editors

Mark Ortman (author of *A Simple Guide to Self-Publishing*) — consultant

All the above, in particular, made suggestions which radically affected this book's development.

Bill Hustead, President, Wall Drug, for commenting on my manuscript and for granting permission to use material from the book *Free Ice Water!*

Jeri Borsch Fahrni and Kevin Wilkins, for information on the South Dakota *coyote* and the geographic center of the United States, respectively

Karen Ufford Campola, Saratoga County Historian, for providing information on Saratoga's history, including the invention of the paper bag

Steve Alexander, the "foremost Custer living historian," for critiquing, supplementing, and generally improving my account of George A. Custer

David E. Ortman, Director, Northwest Office of Friends of the Earth, reviewed my manuscript, then encouraged me by advising, "Hey, these are tourists you're insulting, not terrorists. Go for it."

Linda Seaman, Patterson Printers, for technical advice on printing

Jack Couffer, whose photograph of a pygmy mammoth excavation in Channel Islands National Park on Pearl Harbor Day sometimes seems to be the only thing that unifies this book

Members of the North American Vexillological Association, who have taught me so much about flags

Several National Park Service personnel contributed material and/or offered advice. Special thanks to Richard Beresford and Neal Bullington, who overwhelmed me with material from Saratoga National Historical Park and Capulin Volcano National Monument, respectively, and to those who anonymously overwhelmed me with material from Channel Islands National Park, Craters of the Moon National Monument, the USS *Arizona* Memorial, and Yellowstone National Park. Other contributors are cited with their contributions, unless they requested anonymity. I will be happy to give credit in subsequent printings if so advised. I thank personnel at Carlsbad Caverns and Petrified Forest national parks for critiquing those accounts.

Photo and illustration credits are listed on page 4. I offer special thanks to Ben Garrison, who executed most of the cartoons that appear in this book.

Administered by the National Park Service, Mt. Rushmore National Memorial is a famous unfinished shrine to democracy located near the geographic center of the United States in South Dakota. The sculpture honors, from left to right, the father of our country and surveyor of Virginia's Great Dismal Swamp, the greatest naturalist to ever inhabit the White House, the most accomplished big-game hunter to ever stalk the White House, and the president who took steps to preserve the fabulous valley we call Yosemite even before Yellowstone National Park was established. It was the latter's Secretary of State who purchased America's greatest wilderness preserve — Alaska. George Washington, Thomas Jefferson, and Abraham Lincoln also played pivotal roles in creating the nation's geographic center and maneuvering it towards its present location near Belle Fourche, South Dakota, while Theodore Roosevelt spent some of the wildest years of his wild life hunting wildlife not far north of the site.

An *Evergreen State* Mt. Rushmore?

Pictured above is the author's conception of a mountain in the Cascades of Washington State carved into a shrine similar to Mt. Rushmore. George Washington is replaced by Washington's state flag, which depicts George Washington, for whom the state is so admirably named. A Jefferson ground sloth, Roosevelt elk, and Lincoln mole — all candidates for adoption as Washington State symbols — are used in lieu of the other former presidents. To celebrate America's cultural diversity, a likeness of Crazy Horse could be added. Unfortunately, Crazy Horse didn't live in the Pacific Northwest however.

Alaska — Where women are men and presidents win Iditarods.

Next to Canada, Alaska is America's largest and wildest wilderness preserve. Its addition to our roster of states helped maneuver the geographic center of the United States towards its present location in South Dakota. For both of these blessings, we can thank Abraham Lincoln, for it was his Secretary of State who engineered the purchase of Alaska from Russia in 1867. Unfortunately, Lincoln never had a chance to visit Alaska as he was assassinated two years before the United States took possession. One can only wonder what Lincoln's life would have been like if he had been born and raised in Alaska.

TABLE OF CONTENTS

One of the most familiar symbols of America's national parks, Old Faithful is living proof that fact can be stranger than fiction. The geyser erupts every year on March 1, the anniversary of Yellowstone's establishment as the world's first national park.

HOW TO LOSE — OR USE AND ABUSE — THIS BOOK

In the last paragraph of the Introduction to his wilderness classic, *Desert Solitaire*, Edward Abbey — who was distraught over America's vanishing wilderness — described his book as an "... elegy. A memorial. . . . a tombstone. . . . a bloody rock," adding, "Don't drop it on your foot — throw it at something big and glassy.* What do you have to lose?"

Guess what: America's wilderness is still vanishing. The astonishing questions and remarks in this book are evidence of the corresponding increase in environmental illiteracy that afflicts our increasingly urban nation. Does that mean you should throw this book away? Not necessarily. You can burn it, or find another way of recycling it.

If You Decide to Keep This Book...

In his poem *The Road Not Taken*, Robert Frost — President John F. Kennedy's favorite poet — reminisced about his encounter with a forked road in a "yellow wood." (The yellow was likely evidence of industrial pollution.) After choosing his route, walking along it, and returning home, Frost began philosophizing about the preceding events. He rationalized his choice by noting that he had chosen the least-traveled route, which "made all the difference."

One cannot help but suspect that Frost was just a bit curious about the road he had snubbed. What secrets did it harbor? Was it more beautiful than the path he had taken? Where did it lead?

This is an example of the laziness that pervades our society. Why didn't Frost just go back and hike the damned road he had ignored, rather than dismiss his sloth with a flurry of philosophizing in front of the entire nation? His actions — or inactions — are especially disgusting when one considers that JFK, who did so much to publicize Frost's poetry, was such a physical fitness buff and outdoorsman.

---

*Tourists: Don't take this literally. If you break a window in a national park, you can be charged with destroying government property. The fine can greatly exceed the cost of the broken window.

Don't be a Robert Frost. If you elect to keep this book, then get off your butt and explore America's backcountry, taking it along as a spiritual guide. Don't philosophize about roads not taken — take them all. And take advantage of the book's *interactive* nature.

Interactive means *thinking*. What does the loss of wilderness mean to America? Can we tolerate bureaucracy any longer? Should we break a grand old American tradition and create sensible state flags? Should we carve a mountain in the Black Hills of South Dakota into a shrine honoring women? And if we do, should we let women visit it?

Interactive also means *doing*. Lobby for the adoption of an attractive state flag that celebrates wilderness and diversity. Carry it through the backcountry of a wilderness preserve and plant it in the White House lawn. Throw copies of this book at bureaucrats who dump taxpayers' money — money that could be spent on endangered insects — into a bureaucratic black hole. Mail a copy to a politician in Washington, D.C., thanking him or her for all he or she has done to support the National Park Service and public education, thereby combatting cultural and environmental illiteracy.

Take this book into the wilderness and let it soak up sunshine and morning dew. Carry it up a mountain and drop it into the Grand Canyon. Take it hang-gliding, bungee jumping, and roller-skating in a buffalo herd. Let rodents gnaw on it and throw it at a pesky crow. Bring it home stained with pine resin, coyote urine, beer, sweat, and tears. Then when you pull it off a shelf, you will awaken your senses — and perhaps your neighbors — as well as memories of roads that *were* taken. (Caution: Make sure you haven't grabbed a friend's copy before you take it outdoors and trash it.)

P.S. This book makes a great gift. Buy a copy for a friend so they can throw it away, also. Environmental educators who plan on throwing away or burning large quantities may be eligible for bulk discounts.

INTRODUCTION

I've never been a tourist. But I once came close.

It happened in the wilderness of Katmai National Park, Alaska in 1979. I had cut my first year of college short to work at a cannery in Naknek, a tiny community on the Alaska Peninsula. (I remember a colleague excitedly reporting a fist fight that occurred in our barracks. "I think more than one person was involved!" he exclaimed.)

From Naknek I saw the distant peaks of Katmai, which had seemed to me a fairy-tale place ever since I read about the eruption of Mt. Katmai and the resultant Valley of 10,000 Smokes as a kid. The peaks beckoned me — "Come visit us, David." When I was through canning salmon I went to King Salmon, the gateway to Katmai.

Looking for a place to spend the night, my companions and I wound up at a disco on an Air Force base ("Get Down Tonight..."). Our rustic Alaskan interlude was rudely interrupted when someone questioned our presence. With neither permission to be on base nor a sponsor, we dispersed and sneaked off in the darkness...

and into a bar. It was peaceful, with just two patrons besides my group. They were dancing as we dozed off in our comfortable wooden chairs. Suddenly I was awake. This was no social dance; it was Alaska's unofficial dance, the drunken stupor wrestling match/fist fight — *Welcome to Alaska, where men are men...* When one dance partner came crashing into our table we scurried off in search of new quarters.

Enough culture! While flying into Katmai the next day, I saw my first brown bear on the tundra below.* Upon landing on Naknek Lake at Brooks Camp, I thrilled to the sight of another brown bear running along the beach. It wasn't running from us, however. At Brooks Camp, tourists ran from the bears, which had the run of the place.

I sympathized with the rangers who had to keep bears away from anglers and photographers away from bears. And the comments and

---

*Ursus horribilis. This species, which inhabits North America and Eurasia, is sometimes called a grizzly bear. The huge specimens that frequent Alaska's coastal areas are generally referred to as brown bears or "brownies."

questions! A woman who had just compared a baby moose, one of Nature's gangliest creatures, to the Madonna asked a ranger, "Do the beavers like the cold water?" All the ranger could manage was a feeble, "Uh, I guess so..."

It was at Katmai that I made a tourist-like mistake. I stored food in my tent. It was stored in unopened cans and plastic containers, something a bear could not smell. But it did.

After shredding my tent and taking a bite out of my sleeping pad, the bear ran off, encouraged by a blast from a shotgun wielded by a Park Ranger, Bud Rice. (He fired a nonlethal charge rather than a bullet.) It was an embarrassing beginning for a budding wildlife biologist. Unlike many who err in the wilds, I was offered a second chance — I had another tent.

Bud didn't revoke his previous invitation to accompany him on backcountry patrol in the Valley of 10,000 Smokes, a trip I had at first planned on making alone. My first wilderness experience was enhanced when a third party invited himself along.

Like me, he was young and adventurous. He was also a tourist. Moreover, he was obnoxious, with a voice like Danny Thomas' daughter Marla (Phil Donahue's wife). Do you have any idea what it's like to trek through a pristine wilderness listening to Marla Thomas screeching?*

The Valley of 10,000 Smokes is now smokeless, with just acres and acres of volcanic ash. One evening we watched the sunset from Baked Mountain. It looked like a *Valley of Fire*.

Another unearthly phenomenon I witnessed was the ghastly shrieking of our guest, whose self-standing tent was being blown towards a precipice another evening. Miraculously, the wind blew it past me, and I grabbed it before it disappeared into the abyss. My kindness was rewarded the next evening when our guest announced that he wouldn't bother putting up his tent; he would sleep with me.

---

*I'm referring to the voice that viewers of the unforgettable TV program *That Girl* heard. For all I know, Ms. Thomas, Donahue, or Thomas-Donahue may talk like a normal person in real life.

In the peaceful semidarkness of an Alaskan summer night, my heart thrilled to the musical sound of a brook, accented with the calls of rock ptarmigan. My private wilderness sonata suddenly exploded into a backcountry carnival tune as my companion delivered an off-cue fanfare *à la flatulence*. (Behold, The Valley of 10,000 Smokes lives again!) Was it the falafel he had eaten, after introducing a new word into my vocabulary? Then he began talking in his sleep as his hand crawled across my face. Was some alien dimension using this mystical being to advertise multimedia, more than a decade before the computer industry made it a common feature in Americans' homes?

Upon arriving at a glacier, Bud suggested that *The Music Man* return to Brooks Camp, as he had no ice axe or crampons. (Crampons are metal spikes that can be strapped on to boots, making it possible to walk safely on ice.) "Oh, I don't know," our comrade whined, "I think I'll just hang out with you guys."

We came to a stream. Bud and I took off our packs, sat down, and began taking off our shoes and socks. Our stoic comrade took a shoe off while standing on one foot — and with his pack on! While wrestling with his sock he lost his balance and took a frantic step forward — and steeply downslope. Gravity dictated that he take another step, then another and another. He ran down to the stream and crashed on across, with just one shoe on. ("He can dance, too!" I thought.) I threw his other shoe to him.

Bud led us across the glacier, with me tied in to the other end of the rope. Our multi-talented comrade was tied securely in the middle, slipping and sliding on the ice. We navigated the glacier without incident, returned to Brooks Camp, and parted company.

I survived the humiliation of having my tent destroyed by a brown bear and went on to work for the Alaska Department of Fish and Game, the U.S. Fish and Wildlife Service, the North Slope Borough Environmental Protection Office, and the National Park Service. Bud has done even better, having held a steady job with the National Park Service to this day. The man we dragged over the glacier will, in all likelihood, never be anything more than a gifted tourist.

DEFINITIONS

The following definitions will help readers understand the differences between the various "units" mentioned in this book.

UNITS THAT FOCUS ON NATURE

National parks are generally large and protect diverse resources.

National monuments are generally smaller than national parks and boast less diverse resources. An example is the nation's first national monument, Wyoming's Devils Tower, which showcases an enormous volcanic plug. The Washington Monument is an example of a national monument that celebrates culture rather than Nature.

National preserves are established primarily for the protection of certain resources. In contrast to national parks and monuments, hunting and mining may be allowed if they don't jeopardize natural values. Florida's Big Cypress and Texas' Big Thicket were established as the first national preserves in 1974.

National reserves are similar to national preserves but are managed by local or state authorities. The first national reserve, City of Rocks, Idaho, was established in 1988.

National seashores border the sea. They typically emphasize water-oriented recreation along with the protection of Nature.

National lakeshores — all four of them — border the Great Lakes.

National rivers and **wild and scenic riverways** preserve slender ribbons of land bordering rivers and streams that have not been dammed, redirected, or otherwise improved by the Army Corps of Engineers or other groups.

National scenic trails are paths along which people can hike for great distances through areas of natural beauty.

National forests are administered by the USDA Forest Service. They are frequently managed to strike a balance between wilderness preservation, recreation, and timber farming. (Note: Petrified Forest National Park is a national *park* administered by the National Park Service.)

National wildlife refuges are administered by the U.S. Fish and Wildlife Service (USFWS). With some spectacular exceptions in Alaska and the Southwest, they are typically much smaller than national parks and are not known for their scenic value.

UNITS THAT FOCUS ON CULTURE

Units that celebrate culture include national historic sites, military parks, battlefield parks, battlefield sites, battlefields, historical parks, and a lone international historic site. Wild and scenic rivers find their counterpart in national parkways, ribbons of land flanking roadways — not necessarily unmodified by human agency. While navigating these free-flowing roadways, visitors can search for still more units administered by the National Park Service, including the Wolf Trap Farm Park for the Performing Arts (Virginia) and the John F. Kennedy Center for the Performing Arts (Washington, D.C.). There is even a National Mall in Washington, D.C. It isn't a real mall however, but a landscaped park.

UNITS THAT UNITE NATURE AND CULTURE

National Recreation Areas originally surrounded reservoirs impounded by dams. Today, they encompass a variety of lands and waters set aside for recreational use. Some national recreation areas are managed by the USDA Forest Service.

NATIONAL ABSTRACTIONS

Such things as the *National Debt* are not units but abstract ideas. There are numerous physical objects that can be considered monuments to America's national debt, but none have been officially designated as such.* The only national park or monument proper that celebrates something intangible is probably Arizona's Petrified Forest National Park.

CONCESSIONS

Concessions are commercial operations that are allowed to operate in national parks and other federally (i.e. publicly) owned lands. Concessions sell groceries, gasoline, and souvenirs to visitors and take them river rafting, horseback riding, or llama packing. That concessionaires may be as disoriented as tourists is evidenced by this question that appears on page five of the booklet *National Parks Visitor Facilities and Services*, published by the National Park Hospitality Association: "The National Park System...What are we?" If this book accomplishes nothing besides answering that question, its publication will not have been in vain.

---

*Readers are invited to submit their proposals for national monuments to the National Debt for possible inclusion in a sequel. Send proposals to: National Debt National Monument, Geobopological Survey, PO Box 95465, Seattle, WA 98145

Who says the East is blasé? Located in St. Louis, Missouri, Eero Saarinen's prize-winning, stainless steel Gateway Arch is eerily reminiscent of the stone landforms preserved in Utah's Arches National Park. This arch is symbolic of Thomas Jefferson and other Americans who directed our nation's territorial expansion, as memorialized by Jefferson National Expansion Memorial in St. Louis. By coincidence, Gateway Arch, the most spectacular natural feature between the Missouri River and the Appalachians, is located in the Memorial.

THE EAST
America's Cultural Wilderness

Strange is my name and I'm on strange ground,
And strange it is I can't be found.

The bones of a lost surveyor named Strange were found near a tree in which the above message was carved. A Turkey Run was then renamed Strange Creek according to George Stewart in his classic, *Names on the Land.* The strangest thing of all is that it happened in the East, where there is precious little wilderness to get lost in. But Mr. Strange got lost in the 18th century, when the eastern wilderness was bigger than all of America's present national parks combined.

That there are nine national parks east of the Missouri River today seems more a gesture of compassion than a recognition of genuine wilderness. In my learned opinion, a national park ought to be big enough and wild enough for an adult with moderate outdoors experience to get lost in. Arkansas' Hot Spring National Park's 5,839.24 acres just don't seem adequate. Known more for its therapeutic thermal springs than any floral, faunal, geological, or fossil heritage, this unit is more deserving of the title "National Resort." Michigan's Isle Royale National Park boasts a much more impressive 134,000 acres. But how can anyone get lost on an island?

In the belief that one ought to be able to walk in dignity in a national park, I reject Kentucky's Mammoth Cave and Minnesota's Voyageurs national parks from consideration as quality wilderness. Caves celebrate isolation, not wilderness, subjecting intruders to claustrophobia rather than lifting their spirits with vistas of rock, ice, and sun. And a wilderness that must be navigated by canoe rather than on foot or horseback just doesn't seem American. How many westerns can you remember that were filmed in Voyageurs National Park?

The greatest cluster of eastern national parks, including Mammoth Cave, are in the Appalachians, pathetic remnants of a once proud mountain range. Settled long before the Rockies were explored, the

Appalachians have been grievously strip-mined and long ago purged of elk, bison, wolves, and mountain lions. Great Smoky Mountains (Tennessee/North Carolina) and Shenandoah (Virginia) national parks' floral attractions are truly wondrous — wondrously hardy to survive in the polluted air that engulfs them.

Florida's Everglades National Park is among the most unique units in the system. Its diversity is unexcelled, and what could be wilder than a southern swamp? Unfortunately, Everglades is also the most endangered of our national parks and may even be extinct by the time this book's sequel is finished. (Would readers like that sequel to include some Everglades material anyway? If so, please send me some before Everglades goes under.) Florida's beautiful Biscayne National Park will probably be around until some greedy developer figures out a way to cut off the flow of Atlantic seawater. But it's more of an underwater zoological park than a bona fide American wilderness.

If name recognition is any sort of clue, Acadia National Park is no clue at all. With 41,000 acres, many of them forested, I suppose a number of people could get lost in Acadia. But Yellowstone's 2,220,000 acres — which sprawl over portions of three states — could lose many more. Acadia National Park itself could get lost in Yellowstone.

The East monopolizes National Park Service-sanctioned beaches. The Atlantic Ocean's wild border is commemorated by a series of national seashores, from Massachusetts' Cape Cod and New York's Fire Island to Assateauge Island (Maryland and Virginia), North Carolina's Cape Hatteras and Cape Lookout, Georgia's Cumberland Island, and Florida's Canaveral and Gulf Islands. Inland beaches are protected in Indiana Dunes National Lakeshore, Pictured Rocks and Sleeping Bear Dunes national lakeshores (Michigan), and Apostle Islands National Lakeshore (Wisconsin).

Reality check: Can any seashore or lakeshore in the United States really be considered wilderness? And if not, what are rangers doing there? Can you imagine getting lost in the barren wastes of New York's Fire Island and living off the land and sea for three months until a NASA satellite spots the enormous rescue signals you've gouged in the beach on a winter's day, when the crowds aren't terribly dense?

Ironically, the wildest wildernesses patrolled by Park Rangers east of the nation's mightiest river may well be two units few people have even heard of — Congaree Swamp National Monument, South Carolina and Big Cypress National Preserve, Florida. Congaree Swamp's 22,000 acres may seem paltry, but 22,000 acres of swamp are as efficient at losing people as 100,000 acres of arctic tundra.

With 716,000 acres, Big Cypress represents a healthy chunk of wilderness. (The "Big" in this preserve's name refers to the area, not trees however.) Big Cypress provides freshwater crucial to Everglades National Park. This begs the question, what will become of Big Cypress after Everglades goes under? Will politicians declare it a preserve without a purpose and open it up to settlement by the thousands of immigrants who pour into Florida each year?

While virgin forests are still found here and there in the West, one is fortunate to find a virgin tree farm in the East. Appropriately, this book also reflects an enormous disparity in wilderness-related anecdotes between the two regions.

However, I received an abundance of material relating to the East's vast *urban/suburban* wilderness and to cultural illiteracy. Indeed, writing this book made me realize what windfalls the Revolutionary and Civil wars were for the National Park Service, for many of the eastern units the Park Service oversees commemorate those conflicts. Anyone desiring a job as a Park Ranger in the Northeast is advised to forget horse-packing and ice-climbing and brush up on Revolutionary War history. Wanna spend a winter in the sunny South? Become a Civil War buff.

This book's sequel will hopefully include questions, quips, and anecdotes from the great wilderness areas of the East, including Acadia, Voyageurs, Everglades, and Hot Springs national parks. In the meantime, test your knowledge of American history: Was Thaddeus Kosciuszko a Viking, American Colonist, Briton, Hessian, Yankee, Rebel, Indian, Native American, or other? The answer is on page 38.

Like a pinnacle carved by Ice Age glaciers, the Washington Monument towers over Washington, D.C. While visitors flock to this obelisk and other stone monuments in our nation's capital, scientists are more interested in the surrounding bureaucratic ecosystem which consumes more wood pulp than all of North America's beavers and woodpeckers combined. D.C. is continually swamped with tidal waves of money which mysteriously disappear. This phenomenon reminds scientists of Appalachian rivers that vanish underground as they dissolve limestone. Under intense pressure, limestone metamorphoses into marble, of which many monuments in Washington, D.C. are constructed. Therefore, the Washington Monument might be considered a monument to America's national debt.

THE CULTURAL EAST

DISTRICT OF COLUMBIA
America's Most Dynamic Ecosystem?

With its cultural heritage, the District of Columbia boasts more units administered by the National Park Service than Alaska. Examples include Constitution Gardens, Ford's Theatre National Historic Site, Frederick Douglass National Historic Site, John F. Kennedy Center for the Performing Arts, Lyndon Baines Johnson Memorial Grove on the Potomac, National Capital Parks, National Mall, Pennsylvania Avenue National Historic Site, Rock Creek Park, Theodore Roosevelt Island, Thomas Jefferson Memorial, Vietnam Veterans Memorial, and even the White House.

But the most important National Park Service-related unit in D.C. is the **Department of the Interior**, which oversees the Park Service. In fact, D.C. hosts the headquarters of just about *every* federal agency that manages the nation's natural resources, scenery, rangers, tourists, and unclassified taxpayers. Like Mount Olympus, Capitol Hill towers over this bureaucratic wilderness that sucks up taxpayers' dollars like a black hole and loses them in dimensions that even rangers can't patrol. Socio-ecologists consider the National Park Service an anomaly, describing Park Rangers as "the federal bureaucracy's best bargain." It is eminently logical to support the National Park Service. Therefore, politicians will likely seek ways to eliminate it.

A dominant feature of Capitol Hill is the **Washington Monument**, a 555-foot obelisk that honors George Washington. It recalls an era when Americans were just experimenting with bureaucracy. Park Ranger John Fiedor contributes this anecdote.

My most embarrassing moment as a park ranger was in 1977, while working in front of the entrance to the Washington Monument. Those that work there quickly realize that skills in crowd control are mandatory. As a young, strapping public servant I enjoyed the designated position of "point position" ranger.

26 Ranger Assaults Old Woman in Nation's Capital

One day I was out in front of the monument calmly observing the onrush of six bus loads of visitors charging up the slight hill to the front entrance, each group intent on being the first to crest the slope. It was my job to organize the mob, and I steeled myself silently. Standing tall (halfway to thirteen feet) and resolute, the mob quickly encircled me, filling the air with eager questions and the primeval screams of youth groups. I quickly fielded question after question, gesticulating swiftly the location of the restrooms, snack bar, end of the line for the monument tour, etc. etc.

Minutes passed as hunks of crowd made off at my directions. My confidence growing, I was in firm control when it happened. "Where are the restrooms?" reached my ear and my reaction was swift. The words formed in my head, my mouth opened. To point, I quickly raised my right arm up...THUNK!

An audible gasp from the crowd stayed in the air. They backed off like ripples on a pond. I spun (upon completing the follow through with my right arm) only to see a small gray-haired figure, her jaw leaving my back-hand, arching high into the air away from me. The slight form, in lace and blue dress, landed on her back about six feet away. Immediately her arms and legs started scrambling like an upturned turtle. The only sound for miles was the choking sound of me trying to swallow my heart. Even the kids stopped screaming.

In an instant I was at her side helping her with stammering, sorrowful dialect. Thank God! She was unhurt, and she was apologizing profusely! I helped her to a nearby bench and we talked for several minutes (as I made sure she was okay).

She was delightful! This lovely, 92 year-young lady had seen me from behind as I worked the group. My voice attracted her and she simply had to peek around to see my face. She said she enjoyed my look of terror.

THE HISTORIC NORTHEAST
& America's First Tourists

Are you looking for the ultimate Northeast wilderness adventure? Visit Maine's Acadia National Park, hike to Mt. Katahdin — Maine's highest peak — climb to the summit, and spend the night. In the morning, you will be the first American to see the rising sun. Let a friend photograph you holding this book as it soaks up those first rays. Send me a copy, then paste the original in the book. (Who knows, your picture may appear in the sequel!)

Then you can embark on the ultimate Northeast wilderness adventure. Kayak to Newfoundland, chop down some trees, and build a replica of a Viking ship. (If you have any questions, search for "Heyerdahl, Thor" in a local library's card catalog. He built just about every type of primitive ship known to man.) Next, go to a local bookstore and buy a copy of Farley Mowat's *A Whale for the Killing*, based on an event that occurred in Newfoundland. (Incidentally, I was stationed at Argentia, Newfoundland while in the Navy. It was there that I learned how to play hockey, the national pastime of Canada, the United States' largest wilderness preserve.)

Then persuade some *Newfie* cod-fishermen to help you navigate the stormy North Atlantic in your dragon-boat. When you arrive in Norway, throw a copy of Mowat's book at a local dignitary and ask him why Norwegians are still whaling. Then ask him to autograph my book, noting that Norwegians were America's first European tourists, Vikings having visited Newfoundland some 1,000 years ago.

The idea that early American colonists cared nothing about conservation is a myth. In fact, one of the most popular Revolutionary War flag motifs implored the British to be sensitive to native fauna as they marched from village to village, killing Americans. The coiled rattlesnake appeared on a variety of flags, even going to sea on the famed Gadsden flag, pictured above. Flags pleading for the conservation of flowers evolved into designs carried by American troops in the War of 1812 which admonished, "Don't Walk on Our Grass!" By World War II, American emblems were asking enemies of the Republic to "Take Only Pictures, Leave Only Footprints."

THE REVOLUTIONARY WAR
Could It Happen Again?

Do you know what happened at Saratoga? One of America's contributions to the world of nutrition came about after a spoiled rich person — a Vanderbilt — complained about his potatoes at Moon's Lake House in Saratoga Lake. Slicing the potatoes thinner, the chef produced the first potato chips, which were called Saratoga chips. (There are variations of this story.) The paper bag was invented at nearby Ballston Spa, and two brothers from Saratoga County were the first to successfully commercially market rolls of toilet paper.

But **Saratoga National Historical Park**, at Stillwater, commemorates something that happened before there were paper bags to carry potato chips and toilet paper home in. Here's a hint: It was related to the Revolutionary War. "What was the Revolutionary War?"

Very briefly, the Revolutionary War broke out largely because citizens were tired of being overtaxed by a distant, unfeeling, bureaucratic government. Making matters worse was the fact that the taxes weren't used to help taxpayers. That far-off government just raked 'em in and squandered 'em on bureaucracy, tax-enforcement, and political perks. Sound familiar?

In fact, we may be headed for another Revolutionary War. That's a terrifying thought, considering that the first Revolution resulted in... Hmmm... Who won the Revolutionary War? You should be able to figure it out by the time you get to the chapter on Hawaii.

The material on the following pages was sent to me by Richard Beresford, Museum Technician at Saratoga National Historical Park. He says, "We are often confused with the New York State operated Saratoga Spa State Park, which has a swimming pool, golf course and mineral springs."

Judging by the questions that follow, Saratoga Park is confused with other continents and dimensions. Most of this material is gleaned from Richard Beresford's column, "Heard at the Front Desk," which appears in *The Battlements*, Saratoga Park's newsletter.

What War Was This?

Visitor: So who fought here?
Ranger: The Patriots stopped Burgoyne from Marching to Albany.
Visitor: This Burgoyne — did he fight the Yankees?
Ranger: Well, Burgoyne was British and the "Yankees" were the Revolutionaries. They were called Patriots, but the British called them "Rebels."
Visitor: Oh yes. Now I understand...But what on earth were they fighting about? And who won?

Visitor: So what were they fighting for?
Ranger: American independence.
Visitor: Oh, that's nice — I guess.

Two visitors talking: Where did the Revolutionary War start?
Answer: Canada.

The other day I was explaining to a party, briefly the history of the battlefield and the battle and after I had finished, a well dressed, apparently intelligent woman asked me if I had participated in the battle.

You know, this is one of the nicest and best kept Civil War sites we have been to, and the film was good too!

Grandmother to children: Now here's a postcard that shows the Confederates.

You know my husband and I love the Battlefield. Now my husband really likes it because he found out his grandfather played the drum there all through the Civil War.

A couple came in and said that Saratoga reminded them of Antietam, where there was also fighting. "So, who were the good guys here? Did we win?" After seeing the movie and looking at the brochure, they said, "If George the third spoke English instead of German, we would not have to fight."

Couple looking at books in the bookstore: Guildford Courthouse! Remember how we loved Connecticut!*

---

*Author's note: Guildford Courthouse National Military Park is in North Carolina. It commemorates the battle that opened the campaign leading to Yorktown and the end of the Revolution.

Just answer a question for me. I told my friends here that this is where what's his name fought the battle of whachamacallit and defeated that other fellow, and that other guy who became a spy or something, was a big deal here with a cannon or something. Am I right?

Our biggest naval victory (of the Revolution) was when what's-his-name sank the what do you call it.

Let me understand this straight. I just saw the film and I see that the British and Americans fought the Germans here. Right?

Caller: We would like to be there when you reenact the entire battle of Saratoga. You know, when the men come up from the Hudson and creep through the trees. This is what we want to see.
Ranger: Well, we don't do that here. They have some reenactment at Civil War sites, but we don't.
Caller: Can't take it personally. Is it your fault the Civil War was not fought there? No. So you got stuck with the Revolution, don't feel bad. By the way, what are the big days for you folks?
Ranger: We have a good Independence Day event. We read the Declaration of Independence. We have a musket drill and Liberty Poll.
Caller: That's a hot one. That's good!
Ranger: And then we always have something around the time of the two battles...
Caller: That's good. Very important and good. Do me a favor? Send me a list of your events. We are into the Civil War, but who knows?

Soldiers, Weapons, and Tactics

It says that the enemy forces were defeated by a larger American force, but the figures in the display are the same size!

Visitor: How many people were here?
Ranger: About 33,000.
Visitor to friend: Well, I wasn't close with 50.

It says the British surrendered 12 pound and 24 pound cannons. I think the little one weighs 12 pounds and the big one 24.

I would like to see the musket firing up close but I don't want to hear them. Where should I stand?

When they fired the big cannons, did they hurt anybody?

Boy looking at Breyman Redoubt diorama: Are those blue coats dead?
Mother: No. They're just lying down so they don't get blasted.

The Battle Site

This place is hard to find. Why don't you suggest they move it so people could get here easier?

How did the British find this place? It took us an hour and a half from the Northway!

What a view!! No wonder they had the battle here!

Between us, which way did they come here? By boat or the road?

Sometime ago, a lady with a chauffeur and an expensive car drove up, seemed very much interested and wanted to know where the American Army and where the British Army came from. She was told the road from Quebec, Lake Champlain and the Hudson Valley and then made the remark, "How did they get past the Custom Officer at Rouses Point?"

Visitor: Is there a reason you didn't build this place near the New York State Throughway? Who can find you over here?
Answer: The British did in 1777.

Celebrities

Just between us, what really made [Benedict] Arnold change sides?

Visitor: Where in the park is the monument of Benedict Arnold sitting backwards on a horse?

I brought the grandkids here to learn all about Davy Crockett and Daniel Boone!

Visitor: Who was the American general here?
Ranger: General Horatio Gates.
Visitor to friend: That's what I said.
Friend: No . . . you said let's go through this gate.

Kosciusczko! He came up here after he finished the bridge down in the city, right?

Showing a group through the Schuyler House, the guide points to the painting of General Schuyler and says: Who do you think that is? He lived in this house.
Reply: Oh it's that guy, ah, Shakespeare!

In speaking with two young boys who asked the size of the battlefield, I explained where the camps were and pointed to the ravines that separate them. The smallest one asked "Is that where we can see the headless horseman?"

At the Annual Meeting of the Monument Association in August, 1891, Mrs. Ellen Hardin Walworth, a founder of the Daughters of the American Revolution, gave her report as Chairman of the Committee on the Custody of the Monument. One of the items we found of interest was the following:

"We would recommend that as soon as practicable, the names of Generals Schuyler, Gates, Morgan, and Arnold should be cut in the stone base under the three statues, and under the vacant niche where Arnold's statue would be but for his treason; there are visitors unfortunately ignorant enough to read the names of the sculptures and believe them to be the heroes of the Revolution instead of eminent artists of today."

Burials

Visitor: Do you have to be dead to go to the new cemetery?
Ranger: No. But it would sure move you to the top of the list!

How many unknown soldiers are buried here?

Do you still look for dead people around here?

At the Schuyler House...
Visitor: Are the Schuylers buried here?
Ranger: No.
Visitor: Well are their pets buried here?

So they buried his leg here? Which one? (Benedict Arnold suffered a wounded leg in battle on October 7, 1777. An operation was performed and his leg was saved, but he walked with a limp and endured a great deal of pain. He is buried, leg and all, in England.)

Wildlife

Are you worried about Grizzly Bear here?

Has anyone told you that there are big bear tracks on the hiking trail and also little bear tracks? Do you have any bears?

We honked our horn and turned on the lights but no deer came out. Don't you have deer anymore?

They say American eagles have moved here from New York City? Do you know what made them leave town?

Why do you have so many birds here and we don't back home?

How many of the wild deer are tame?

Dinosaurs

I see that you have ten stops on the tour road, which is nice, but where are the dinosaur tracks?

Do you still have the big dinosaur tracks around here? They were on one of the steps outside.

Atmospheric Phenomena

Visitor: Why didn't you warn us about the thunderstorm!
Ranger: Didn't the other Ranger just warn you about the thunder?
Visitor: Yes, but you didn't!

Q: When do you start cross country skiing around here?
A: When it snows.
Q: When do you end cross country skiing?
A: When it stops snowing.
Q: When is that??

This may seem like a funny question, but there is snow on the lawn. Does that mean there is snow on the trails too?

Hiking

We want to take a walk and see some scenery. What would you suggest?
Ranger: We have a very nice trail called the Wilkinson Trail. It is 4.2 miles and covers a lot of the battlefield. It starts just beyond the sign out there on the front lawn.
Does the scenery start there, too?

After hiking: We think we will come back after the mud slides are over.

How long is the Wilkinson hiking trail?
Ranger: It is 4 ½ miles around.
If we only walk half way out and come back, how far would that be?

Films

It certainly gave me a better understanding of the Civil War.

How long is the 20 minute film?

Q: Would you like to see our film?
A: No thanks. We saw one at Gettysburg.

Would you like to see our film?
What's it about?
It's about 20 minutes.

On leaving the film: Sometimes the film is very good.

Miscellaneous Attractions

Which water slide do you suggest we try first?

Is there a reason why I can't ride my bike on the hiking trail?

Is there a special place for swimming in the battlefield?

Time

What time is the Eastern sunrise service?

Is the astronomy walk at night?

Rangers

Ranger: We have two interpreters at the Neilson House today.
Visitor: What languages are they interpreting?

Visitor: Is this place part of the National Park Service?
Ranger: Yes
Visitor: Well, if it really is, why don't they serve coffee?

At the end of the winter skiing season a visitor came by and said, "I am sure you hate to see this end. What kind of job will you get for the summer?"

Miscellaneous

Ranger: Would you like a brochure?
Visitor: No — we want to look around before we get into that.

I don't know where we came from; I don't know where we are going. Can you help me?

Visitor to friend: Well, we have to buy an insipid post card. Look they have some over here!

Your sign says "62 or over? Visit every park free. Ask for details." The two of us combined comes to over 62. Does that count?

A visitor showing friends one of the exhibits: It is very important to remember that a Redoubt is a hill with a picket fence on top!

Children's Questions

Why didn't Burgoyne come down the Northway from Canada to Albany?

Gee. You had to brush your teeth even then!

(Continued on page 38)

In the mid-18th century, Irish pirates were smuggling millions of tons of potatoes — many of them stolen from British soil — to the American colonies, where they were made into Saratoga chips. Infuriated, the British planned a three-pronged invasion — by land, sea, and air. However, ships could not reach landlocked Saratoga, while bad weather kept British planes on the ground. The site was difficult to find on the ground, but a spy infiltrated Saratoga, leaving a trail of toilet paper so that he could find his way back. The British thought it was a signal to follow and attack. Foolishly, Shakespeare committed his infantry without the support of his fleet and air force. The Confederates, led by Davy Crockett, Daniel Boone, and Theodore Roosevelt,

drove the smaller British forces, led by the Headless Horseman, out of the dinosaur tracks in which they had sought refuge. German allies blocked the British from commandeering the ski slopes. A hero of the battle, Benedict Arnold later became a traitor and led the British against the Alamo, where Davy Crockett was killed. Daniel Boone met his Waterloo at the Battle of Waterloo in Montana after refusing to accept Crazy Horse's offer to cease hostilities if Mt. Rushmore was returned to the Sioux nation. Alarmed that the British had managed to penetrate Saratoga's potato fields, Thomas Jefferson engineered the Louisiana Purchase and relocated Saratoga's potato chip industry to Idaho. The rest is history.

At the Neilson House a boy from a school group looked at the fire pit being maintained by a person in 18th Century costume and asked: Is that fire gas operated?

A four year old pointing to a display case: And that's where they keep the battleships.

A little boy approached a Ranger after looking at all the exhibit cases. Pointing to a case with a topographical map, he asked: Is that your ant farm?

Family leaving the Visitor Center with information that an ancestor had fought with the 2nd New Hampshire Regiment: But mom are we related to the father or the son?

Dear Friends:

I am a fifth grade student. My teacher is making me write this letter. It is not your fault.

Can you please send me some information about your park so I can get credit in school and study about it?

Thank you!

****

On October 7, 1777, General John Burgoyne (British) and General Horatio Gates (American) clashed at Freeman's Farm (Saratoga). When the fighting ended at dusk, Burgoyne counted 700 casualties, Gates no more than 150. Burgoyne retreated to Saratoga (now Schuylerville) where he and his army of 5,000 surrendered to Gates on October 17. The American victory ended British plans to reduce New England and induced France to join the war as an ally of the United States. The battle is considered a turning point in the Revolution and one of the decisive battles of world history. Major General Philip Schuyler's country home and the 154-foot Saratoga monument are nearby.

The National Park Service administers a Thaddeus Kosciuszko National Memorial at 301 Pine Street, Philadelphia, which commemorates the life and work of this Polish-born patriot and hero of the American Revolution.

****

The suffering poorly equipped American troops endured while en-camped in Valley Forge, Pennsylvania during the winter of 1777-1778 is legendary. **Valley Forge National Historical Park** contains General George Washington's headquarters, original earthworks, a variety of monuments and markers, and recreations of log buildings and cannon. A ranger who worked here said he encountered a visitor who couldn't understand why Washington and his troops were so poorly supplied and hungry when they were camped so close to a railroad.

This painting of George Washington crossing the Delaware is perhaps the most famous painting that celebrates the Revolutionary War. Unfortunately, it's not entirely accurate. History buffs, can you find the historical inaccuracy? The answer is on page 57.

Flags of Secession

(Top) The Confederate battle flag lives on in the state flags of Georgia, Mississippi, and other states in the South.

(Bottom) Nowhere does the desire for freedom burn stronger than in Michigan, which seceded from itself (see page 57).

THE CIVIL WAR

When Will It End?

You've already read a number of questions and quips relating to the Civil War. They appeared under New York's Saratoga National Historical Park, which commemorates a Revolutionary War battle.

Some 600,000 soldiers died during the four-year Civil War, many more than were lost in Vietnam. When one considers how many fewer people inhabited the United States over a century ago, it becomes apparent how survivors must have been shaken by such staggering losses. Yet the loss of more than half a million Americans pales next to the 3.6 million who were freed from slavery. Truly, the Civil War affected America as no other war.

It was on April 9, 1865 that Confederate General Robert E. Lee surrendered to Union General Ulysses S. Grant at Appomattox, Virginia. Some might argue that the Civil War ended in Alaska, where the last military engagement was fought. (News of surrenders traveled slowly in those days.) I suggest the Civil War hasn't ended at all.

Out of an estimated 10,500 Civil War engagements, 384 battlefield sites are left, one in three of them in Virginia. The Civil War means big business to the National Park Service, which manages thirty-two Civil War-related sites. The five most visited sites are Gettysburg, Pennsylvania (1.4 million per year); Chickamauga, Georgia and Vicksburg, Mississippi (1 million apiece); Kennesaw, Georgia (929,800); and Manassas, Virginia (614,900).

Not content to merely visit battlefield sites, an estimated 20,000 Americans participate in about 300 Civil War battle reenactments each year. Still more people relive the Civil War at home. Visiting the local Bulldog News, a vendor just a few blocks from my residence in Seattle, I noted the following magazines for sale: *Civil War Times*, *The Gettysburg Magazine*, and *Blue & Gray Magazine* ("For Those Who Still Hear the Guns"). "Battle Born," declares the legend on the state flag of Nevada, which became a state while the war was raging. (Don't Nevadans have anything native to celebrate?) It seems somehow incongruous that Abraham Lincoln, who is credited with freeing the slaves, shares his berth on Mt. Rushmore, near the geographic center of the United States, with two presidents who were slave-owners.

Lee's surrender at Appomattox didn't dull Americans' spirit for rebellion. Witness Key West, Florida, whose residents declared themselves an independent *Conch Republic*, and Wounded Knee II. In the Pacific Northwest, dreams of independence have fostered such terms as *Ecotopia*, *Cascadia*, and *Jefferson*. With their reputation for individualism, Alaskans have been known to harbor similar sentiments. Native Hawaiian separatists have adopted their own flag, a striking improvement over the current state flag, which suggests a British colony. Indeed, all good rebellions seem to center around flags.

A great controversy has been raging for some time over Civil War flags, a number of southern states being represented by flags inspired by the Confederate battle flag. The "Confederate swastika" is what some people, particularly African Americans, call this symbol of the Old South. "Nonsense," cries the opposition, "our state flags merely honor our Confederate ancestors!"* A number of groups are committed to changing Southern emblems and there are people outside the South who wish them well. "Let's put those racist, backwards Southerners in their place, once and for all!"

Brace yourself for a California redwood-sized dose of irony: *Most* state flags commemorate the Civil War. Vexillologist (flag expert) Gary Csillaghegyi explains.

Most of our State Flags grew out of the Civil War by adopting the colors of the State Militia as the state flag with little or no modification. That's why so many are so intricate: military colors are that way, beautifully embroidered or painted by a real artist. That is also why most of them are blue, the color of the Infantry. The exceptions on the East coast arose because the militias were Revolution in origin and a different code of colors for the uniforms and such was devised then. New York and New Jersey were both buff (yellow in manufacture), for instance. New York changed its [flag] to blue to match the new Infantry branch color of the Civil War.

*An admirable argument. And since flags are meant to represent all Americans, Southern flags — in my opinion — ought to also honor the ancestors of citizens who did *not* support the Confederacy.

Adding to the irony is the fact that most state flags are inferior in design and appearance to Southern flags. They are extremely complex yet, ironically, not distinctive. Such a monotonous array of flags hardly suggests the cultural and natural diversity that makes America so great.

Still more insulting is the fact that the most blatantly discriminatory emblems are found outside the South. Native Americans are depicted retreating from pioneers on several emblems, for example. Such emblems were eminently appropriate for the era in which they were designed, when slavery was legal, women weren't allowed to vote, and the United States' general policies towards Native Americans, forests, grasslands, and wildlife were eerily similar. Do such emblems have any place in contemporary America?

Considering that most of the eastern United States has been plowed, asphalted, and generally urbanized, the standard state flag design — a blue banner bearing a state seal in the center — is perhaps appropriate. To simplify matters — and save money on manufacturing costs — why don't we just give every state east of the Missouri River a blue banner with the state's name emblazoned across the center?

Many Americans laugh off such ideas as frivolous nonsense — until someone burns an American flag. Then such important issues as poverty, crime, the economy, and the loss of wild species and wilderness are forgotten as citizens, presidential candidates, and Congress frantically grope for ways to protect the *Stars and Stripes* without sacrificing freedom of expression.

According to the April 10, 1995 issue of *U.S. News & World Report*, the most valuable Civil War artifacts are battle flags, which fetch prices of $2,500 to $100,000. The recent discovery that a flag that flew over the Alamo is in the possession of Mexican authorities has whipped Texans into a patriotic frenzy. Flags mean far more to most Americans than they realize.

P.S. After the Civil War, when cotton was in short supply, cotton bags were in short supply. America was ripe for the paper bag, which was invented — remember? — near Saratoga. All things are connected.

The nation's first national military park, **Chickamauga and Chattanooga National Military Park** (Georgia/Tennessee) commemorates a major Confederate victory on Chickamauga Creek in Georgia on September 19-20, 1863. The victory was countered by subsequent Union victories at Orchard Knob, Lookout Mountain, and Missionary Ridge in Chattanooga, Tennessee. A former employee of the Park recalls a visitor's question and her reply.

Why was the Civil War fought in a national park?

"Well it's obvious why, all the cannon were in place, monuments were here to hide behind, and we could make the traffic one-way going in and one-way going out."

Arkansas' **Pea Ridge National Military Park** commemorates a Union victory of March 7-8, 1862. One of the major Civil War engagements west of the Mississippi River, it led to the Union's total control of Missouri.

Here at Pea Ridge National Military Park, off-the-wall visitor queries are not original. Occasionally a visitor may ask "Can you drive on the tour road?" or "Which war is this?" Several people have asked while standing at the register in the bookstore if we have a gift shop. We think this is probably a question of semantics because many people like to buy coffee mugs, pens and T-shirts rather than books. One visitor saw a photo of an alligator on some literature at the front desk and asked if we had alligators in the park.

Fredericksburg and Spotsylvania County Battlefields Memorial National Military Park, Virginia is comprised of portions of four major Civil War Battlefields — Fredericksburg, Chancellorsville, the Wilderness, and Spotsylvania Court House, along with Chatham Manor and several smaller historic sites. Near the park is Fredericksburg National Cemetery, where 15,333 soldiers are interred, 12,746 of them unidentified.

My name is Vincent Kordach, currently a ranger at Boston National Historical Park and during my first summer with the National Park Service at Fredericksburg NMP in 1977, fielded a question which I have never forgotten.

Working at the visitors center desk late one afternoon, a man came inside and approached me. "I'm interested in finding out if an ancestor of mine is buried in the National Cemetery," he said, gesturing with his hands toward Marge Heights. "Yes, those men who were identified are indexed here," I replied, and let him check out the cards. After a few minutes, the man looked up and said, "Well, I don't see the name here. Could you now show me the list for all the unknown men buried in the cemetery?"

Gettysburg National Military Park, Pennsylvania, preserves the site where a Confederate invasion of the North was repulsed on July 1-3, 1863, in the greatest battle ever to occur in North America. Union losses in killed, wounded, or missing were 23,000. The Confederates reported losses of 20,000. Its manpower almost exhausted, the Confederacy could not replace its casualties.

It was at Gettysburg that President Lincoln delivered his famous Gettysburg Address. (Gettysburg, PA 17325 is the Park's address, not the Gettysburg Address.) Park Ranger John Fiedor comments on Gettysburg.

While working the visitor center desk at Gettysburg National Military Park often visitors would run up and ask if they were too late for the next showing of the Electric Map, an orientation program on the battle that uses lights. One gentleman was in such a hurry he blurted out, "Am I too late for the electric chair!" He was too late. But, we got him in (to the map not the chair) after he realized what he had said became rather embarrassed by the laughter of visitors around him.

Of course the one question that was asked a lot at Gettysburg, by young and old alike, required a delicate answer. It seems, after viewing the impressive battleground, that people wanted to know "Were the monuments here at the time of the battle?"

Along similar lines, I read in a newspaper about a Gettysburg guide who reportedly was asked, "Where do you store all the stone monuments in the winter?"

(The Unfinished Civil War is Continued on page 57)

MORE HISTORY
Martin Van Buren & Peanut Butter

Martin Van Buren was our eighth president and one of the principal architects of the Democratic Party. Lindenwald was his retirement home. It has been restored to its appearance during Van Buren's time. The following is contributed by Marion Berntson, Supervisory Park Ranger at **Martin Van Buren National Historic Site** at Kinderhook, New York.

The tours are about 40 minutes long depending on the size and interests of the group. I had a group that seemed to want to fly through the house. I was determined that they would learn something on the tour! As we moved, rapidly through the servants' dining room I said, "The servants were Irish!" That has to be the shortest tour in history!

When many tours are given during a day, sometimes words just don't come out as you planned. For example: When talking about Van Buren's potato crop, it came out potato c-r-a-p; when mentioning that the President's dining table would seat 30, it came out that the table would sleep 30. It is something that happens and the visitors and ranger all have a good laugh.

One day I was about to start my tour, but needed to put my ranger hat into the small closet in the Visitors' Center. I said, obviously a little premature, "Follow me." They did — right into the closet!

****

Booker T. Washington National Monument, Virginia preserves the birthplace and early childhood home of the famous black leader and educator. A correspondent offers the following item.

Certainly some of the most frequently asked questions I receive from visitors include what association Booker T. Washington had with peanut butter. It always does my heart good when I have convinced people that it was George Washington Carver, and not Booker T. Washington, the educator, who was the agriculturalist/botanist. Perhaps the confusion is a result of the names of the two gentlemen; perhaps it is that both worked at Tuskegee Institute in Alabama.

Abraham Lincoln exerted a powerful influence on the West, even though he never traveled west of the Missouri River. An assassin's bullet prevented him from driving the golden spike, thus altering the course of Utah's history (see page 156). Before he was assassinated, however, Lincoln helped preserve the spectacular valley that would later be designated Yosemite National Park. What would Lincoln's life had been like if he had grown up in Yosemite? This picture depicts Lincoln free-climbing Half Dome.

BEYOND HISTORY

Haddonfield National Non-Prehistoric Site?

New Jersey has no national parks or monuments. It is woefully depauperate of even national historic sites despite the nickname *Pathway of the Revolution*. New Jersey shares the Appalachian National Scenic Trail, Delaware National Scenic River, Delaware Water Gap National Recreation Area, Gateway National Recreation Area, and Statue of Liberty with other states. The only National Park Service-administered units New Jersey has all to itself are Edison National Historic Site in West Orange and Morristown National Historical Park, Morristown, which commemorate a great American inventor and the Revolutionary War, respectively.

Haddonfield, New Jersey, is a city that threw away a great opportunity. It's far too small, civilized, and unremarkable to be a national park or monument, but it merits consideration as a national historic site or, more appropriately, a national *prehistoric* site.

When Europeans discovered the first known dinosaur in 1822, people didn't know what to call it; the word "dinosaur" wasn't coined until 1841. The animal, named Iguanodon, was represented by too few bones to be properly reconstructed and was portrayed, incorrectly, as quadrupedal. It was up to Americans to get the budding science of paleontology — and dinosaurs — on a proper footing.

In 1838 huge bones were discovered in a marl pit near Haddonfield and carted off as souvenirs. William Parke Foulke later traced stories about the bones to the forgotten pit. In 1858 he excavated the first nearly complete dinosaur skeleton known to science.

This enigma was a hadrosaur, or duck-billed dinosaur, named *Hadrosaurus foulkii* in its discoverer's honor. The bones obviously represent a bipedal animal. A member of a group of dinosaurs ancestral to duckbills, England's Iguanodon was redesigned accordingly.

Haddonfield's hadrosaur established the United States as a leader in dinosauria even before the West's great dinosaur quarries were discovered. What school would not rejoice at having a *dino-site* of such magnitude in its back yard? *Hadrosaurus foulkii* became New

Jersey's official state dinosaur in 1991, through the efforts of elementary school children from Strawbridge Elementary School. Ironically, Strawbridge School is not in Haddonfield but in Westmont.

But Haddonfield authorities fenced off the discovery site, preserving it for posterity, right? Well, no. Actually, it's now adjacent to the Haddonfield waste water treatment plant.

At least Haddonfield students can see Foulke's hadrosaur in local museums and rejoice in the knowledge that the creature came from their back yard, right? Not quite — the fossils are in the possession of the Academy of National Sciences in Philadelphia, Pennsylvania.

But what are exhausted fossil sites and museums? What's more important are the ideas and knowledge the bones represent. Capitalizing on name similarities, authorities dreamed up *Haddonfield Hadrosaurs* as a nickname for local school groups, right? Wrong. Haddonfield schools sport the nickname *Haddonfield Bulldogs*.

But there's a bright side to this tale of missed opportunities. Haddonfield students can thank the town fathers for not giving them a nickname that is totally stupid, like the *Haddonfield Huckleberries*, or the *Haddonfield Hyenas*. Bulldogs are, after all, kind of neat. I guess. Go Bulldogs!

THE NATURAL EAST

SEASHORES & 1 LAKESHORE
A Treasury of Coastal Humor

Remember that stuff I wrote earlier about national seashores not being wild enough for people to get lost in? I was wrong! A Park Ranger recalls being asked by a "very well-dressed couple" at Massachusetts' **Cape Cod National Seashore** where Providence was.

I asked if they meant Providence, R.I., or Provincetown, here on Cape Cod. "No, Rhode Island. We drove from New York City and we are supposed to be at a wedding in 20 minutes." Which means they had driven right through Providence about two hours before.

(Continued on page 52)

RIVERS & CAVES
(Well, Two of Them)

The New River is among the continent's *oldest* rivers. This rugged, whitewater river flows through deep canyons, the 52-mile section from Hinton to Fayetteville being abundant in natural, scenic, historic, and recreational features. A ranger offers some material relating to **New River Gorge National River**, West Virginia.

"Why are those rocks moving?" They ask this when first setting out in a raft, not realizing yet that it is they that are in motion!

"How long does it take for a small rock to grow into a boulder?"

"Will we end up back where we started?" (on a whitewater rafting trip) Many visitors are from flat places and are not aware that floating down a river means ending up in a much lower place than where the trip starts. They think of it more like an amusement park ride where you start and end at the same place.

A Treasury of Coastal Humor
(Continued from page 51)

A visitor to Florida's **Gulf Islands National Seashore** asked, while standing on one of the islands, "Where is the beach?" This unit also boasts historic forts whose defenders are not forgotten. According to a correspondent, "A young student called in and wanted to speak to someone who was at Fort Pickens in 1861."

Within the borders of Indiana, a state that once deserved its nickname *Crossroads of America*, lie the sprawling wilds of **Indiana Dunes National Lakeshore**. With its vast stretches of vegetation, beaches, and water, it is easy for people to become disoriented, if not lost here. Indeed, a frequently asked question is "Which beach is closest to the water?" The ranger who contributed that question adds the following:

> One common misperception that visitors have about our park becomes evident whenever a visitor enters our visitor center and asks, "Where are the dunes?" Our response is often, "You're standing on them." We then explain that the visitor center is nestled among the Glenwood dunes, an older, wooded dune system that was formed thousands of years ago when Lake Michigan was at a higher level, and that the younger "big sand dunes" are located at the present beach.

> Another ranger adds the following note.

> Recently, a couple was eating lunch at a picnic table at one of our sites. As I walked by, the man, noting my ranger hat and uniform, asked, "Where's Yogi?" I replied, "Stealing your picnic basket!"

Rivers & Caves (Continued from page 51)

Mammoth Cave National Park is located in Kentucky. It is named for Mammoth Cave, which is within the Park's borders.

With more than 300 miles of underground passages explored and mapped, Mammoth Cave ranks as the longest recorded cave system in the world. The true extent of Mammoth Cave's inky tentacles would be known if there were some way to answer this visitor's question: "How much of the cave is unexplored?"

GO WOLVERINES!
Eastern Wildlife Adventures

Harper's Ferry National Historic Park, West Virginia/Virginia/ Maryland recalls John Brown's raid of 1859. Strategically located at the confluence of the Shenandoah and Potomac rivers, this town changed hands many times during the Civil War. How many groundhogs have changed hands here? The following is contributed by Park Ranger John Fiedor.

Kids can be a wonder at times, particularly if they are curious. Once at Harpers Ferry National Historical Park I was observing from afar one of my favorite interpreters at work, Jeff Ridgeway. He was on the park's green and had a crowd of visitors on the proverbial edge of their seats. Being toward the rear of the crowd I watched as a young boy (recently off-loaded from a bus from the inner city of Washington D.C.) came running up to the group, working his way inward to Mr. Ridgeway. He seemed to have his jacket wrapped around something.

I could not quite hear what was said, but as he confronted Jeff the crowd backed off considerably and quickly. Calmly (based upon his countenance and not any words that I could hear) Jeff pointed for the boy to move outside the crowd, which he did. Further hand signals caused the boy to bend over and open his jacket, from which a rather large ground-hog came leaping out. The ruffled animal took a single, shocked look at the kidnapper, and then bounded as gracefully as a fat rodent could into the nearby woods. Once out of sight the crowd, with the curious young boy, again circled Jeff to listen to his eloquent words.

Great Smoky Mountains National Park (Tennessee/North Carolina) nestles in the loftiest range east of South Dakota's Black Hills. Park Ranger Harry Cook sent me the following anecdote.

In 1992, I was working in the Great Smoky Mountains on Balsam Mountain as a law enforcement ranger. . . . [A] story concerning bears at Balsam Mountain is when a bear was exploring the campground and spotted a can of bug repellent at one site. It went right up and grabbed the can with its mouth and bit into it. Immediately, the can started spraying into the bear's mouth and quickly, the can was dropped and the bear ran to the woods.

The campers whose bug repellent had been stolen by the bear became very worried that the spray would make the bear very sick or even worse. However, that worry didn't last long for about ten minutes later, the bear came out of the woods, grabbed the can again and started licking it. He must have liked the taste.

Located in South Carolina, **Congaree Swamp National Monument**'s 22,200 acres contain a significant tract of southern bottomland hardwood forest and diverse species associated with an alluvial (river) floodplain. The park boasts several national and state record trees. An employee of Congaree Swamp National Monument sent the following letter.

Attached is a true story which occurred at the park several years ago. It is humorous in the fact that it happened to a self-professed expert. It is educational in that it reminds us that if we leave wild animals alone we can avoid injury. This is the only instance we know of a person being bitten by a poisonous snake in the park in the past 14 years.

We prefer to remain anonymous and have deleted references to individuals in the attachment.

SNAKEBITE!!

Four years ago, on a hot June day, Ranger ******** and I were working in the Ranger Station at the front desk. At 1 o'clock a visitor walked in to pick up a trail map and a park brochure.

He immediately struck me as unusual. He wore silver snake rings on each of his fingers. His hat band was a rattlesnake skin. Sewn on his blue jeans were Cobra decals. A picture of a large black Cobra stared at me from the front of his tee-shirt. Black snakes were tattooed on each arm. His first words were "Hi, I'm a snake expert." I was not about to argue with him. He certainly appeared to be a so called snake expert. I gave him a trail map and he proceeded down the service road towards the old clubhouse with a friend.

Two hours later, the "snake expert" was sitting on the front steps of the Ranger Station with his head between his knees. I saw him and noticed something was amiss through the screen door. I asked him if anything was wrong. He said "I've been bitten by a copperhead on my thumb!" I looked and saw his thumb was red and swollen. I dialed "911" for an ambulance, took him into my office and laid him out on the floor with his feet propped up to treat for shock. Meanwhile, Ranger ******** noticed a bag on his bicycle with a shoulder strap on it. She asked his friend. "May I look in the bag?" The friend looked fairly out of sorts at this time. She lifted the bag and unzipped it very slowly. Inside were two live copperhead snakes.

An ambulance arrived within 15 minutes and paramedics treated the bitten thumb by freezing it. A paramedic asked me if I would kill the snake so the doctor could identify it and choose the proper antivenom. I dispatched the snake with a hoe. Both the dead snake and the snake-bitten "snake expert" were carted off to the hospital. Ranger ******** ticketed him for snake poaching. To my knowledge this is the only time that anyone has been bitten by a poisonous snake at the park.

From West Virginia's **New River Gorge National River** come these offerings:

A few years ago there was a rumor that the park service was stocking the park with rattlesnakes! A version of the rumor claimed that wild turkeys were being recruited to incubate rattlesnake eggs. Many people believed this and were very upset. We still get an occasional call about the rattlesnakes.

The park was reintroducing peregrine falcons to the gorge at the time the rumor surfaced, but it is hard to say how all the elements of the snake & turkey tale emerged. Anonymous Please

****

While working for the U.S. Fish and Wildlife Service in Florida, I assisted a biologist in a vegetation survey on St. Vincent Island National Wildlife Refuge, which encompasses, appropriately, St. Vincent Island. All good biologists have some botanical skills, though their specialty may lie in zoology. My supervisor's first love was herpetology — the study of reptiles and amphibians.

Herpetologists are as distinctive as birders (he enjoyed bird-watching, as well). While the latter can be identified at a glance by their binoculars and skyward stares, the hallmarks of herpetologists, who are generally more down to earth, are a gunny sack and rake. Rakes are used in prying apart dead trees or logs, which may harbor "herps."

Anyway, my boss told me a story about a herpetologist who was rummaging around in the woods one day when he spotted a herpetologist's dream: Before him was a dilapidated shack! He immediately attacked the structure with his rake, his eager eyes alert for prey as he tore at the walls.

Suddenly, he broke through... there before him was the sight of a lifetime — a family sitting down to dinner.

I laughed when I heard this story, even as I realized the tragedy. I felt a second twinge of embarrassment as I realized that my first feelings of sympathy went not to the poor family but to the trespassing herpetologist; I suppose it's simply easier to empathize with someone whose shoes I could have easily filled.

In *Desert Solitaire*, Edward Abbey wrote, "The wilderness should be preserved for political reasons," citing the wilderness' value as a refuge from government and industry. The wilderness, Abbey maintained, can be used as a base "for guerilla warfare against tyranny." I agree.

But I think the wilderness — or at least rural areas — are equally important, if not more so, as a simple haven for the downtrodden. I've never been poor. I've been broke on frequent occasions, and have lived fairly close to the threshold of poverty. But I've never truly been poor.

I know, however, that if I had to be poor, I would want to be poor in a rural, rather than urban, environment. In the city, poor people are surrounded by excessive bureaucracy, crime, and garbage, with little inspirational to brighten their lives save church — if they're the religious type — and children, for whose safety, welfare, and future they have little hope.

Rural poor can at least enjoy the dignity of freedom and savor the luxuries of time and peace in an environment where the sun may be observed as it makes its daily journey from horizon to horizon, oblivious to the joys and sorrows of people.

****

Herpetologists are not so common in Michigan, the only state nicknamed for an animal that doesn't live there and apparently never was common. The animal is that living symbol of wilderness, the wolverine (Go Wolverines!). From the earliest days of exploration by Europeans, only a handful of wolverines have been reported in Michigan. (I've read of just one. It's probably safe to assume that its parents at least wandered across the Canadian border from time to time, though.)

Looking at Michigan's flag (see page 40), with its elk and moose, while thinking about wolverines ranks as one of the greatest wildlife adventures that can be experienced today in the civilized East.

The Unfinished Civil War (Continued from page 45)

Civil War monuments are not confined to national parks. Michigan's state flag (see picture on page 40) saw action in the Civil War. (Michigan's flag actually predates the Civil War.)

Michigan's flag is unique in depicting both an elk and moose, which by themselves are featured on a number of state emblems. These don't relate to the Civil War, for elk were pretty much exterminated in the East before the Civil War broke out, while moose range far to the north of Civil War battle sites. Even if the Confederates had captured Washington (D.C.), they wouldn't have dined on moose.

Perhaps it is this Civil War era flag that inspired another Michigan distinction: It apparently seceded from itself. Residents still pay a stiff penalty for their act of treason — Michigan is the only state whose citizens have to drive through another state (Wisconsin) to get to the other half of their state.

Answer to Question on Page 39: There is no smoke! Smokeless energy sources weren't developed until long after the Revolutionary War. Prior to their development, trains were fueled by wood or coal which produced smoke — and lots of it!

The Dakota Territorial seal advertises the region's diverse and abundant natural resources and scenic attractions. The seal depicts a flying jack-a-lope against the Black Hills, with the distant Rocky Mountains behind them and the Himalayas in the background. The artist's inaccurate depiction of Mt. Everest — the highest peak in the design — is understandable when one considers that he never visited the Rocky Mountains, let alone the Himalayas. Ironically, scientists have recently discovered that the jack-a-lope's ancestral home is near the Himalayas.

Now that North and South Dakota have achieved statehood, each state wants the rights to the seal, which an artist from Rapid City claims he can modify into a state seal. A North Dakota rancher who took a class in mathematics and practices law as a hobby has suggested that the seal be divided in two, with each state receiving at least one half. The states are now arguing over who will get the half with the little cow, and there are rumors that a second cow may be added to the design. This might be a good opportunity for budding young artists who want to take a stab at drawing a four-legged animal.

THE DAKOTAS

Still Dividing America

All things are connected — but fortunately not to the Dakotas
Native American proverb

The Dakotas lie between the cultural centers of the East and the great wilderness areas of the West. Millions of Americans have driven across South Dakota enroute to national parks and monuments. Millions of Americans have driven across South Dakota on their way back home. Most of them have avoided North Dakota.

****

North Dakota is as bleak a state as you could ever hope to avoid. Agriculture is not only the main industry — it's the *only* industry. "Strength from the Soil" is North Dakota's official motto. The grooviest personality North Dakota ever produced was that hip Strasburg bandleader, Lawrence Welk.

While other states are represented by the powerful buffalo, grizzly bear, and moose, North Dakota is nicknamed the *Flickertail State* for the ground squirrels that entertain farmers by twitching their tails. (The flickertail has never been officially adopted as the state animal, as no one has figured out how to introduce the bill in the legislature.) You might think North Dakotans are simple-minded — but they aren't.

As a matter of fact, North Dakota boasts some of the nation's most creative, imaginative people. Here's an example: Five states in the South adopted the largemouth bass as their official fish. Various trout and salmon represent more northern states. (Illinois' bluegill designation is as unique as it is stunning.) These and other state fishes were adopted primarily because anglers like to angle for them.

But North Dakotans are not followers — how do you think they got stuck in North Dakota? No, they put some thought into their designation. (With more time on their hands than the rest, North Dakota anglers were able to figure out how to introduce a legislative bill.) They chose the northern pike, capitalizing on the connection between *north*ern pike and *North* Dakota.

North Dakota's state flower, the wild prairie rose, commemorates the grasslands that cover practically the entire state. (Contrary to rumors, North Dakota's highways are frequently grass free.) The state tree, the American elm, is a reminder that North Dakota is a part of America. All North Dakotans need to complete their geographic roster is an official earthworm to remind their children of their native planet. Then school teachers can throw away their geography texts like they've been threatening to do for years.

If North Dakotans ever decide to adopt a state animal, it may be a contest between the flickertail and moose. The latter is a reminder of the Bull Moose Party, of which Theodore Roosevelt was a champion. I propose that the moose be adopted as the mascot of North Dakota's **Theodore Roosevelt National Park**. If Park officials complain that moose don't live there, let's remind them that Theodore Roosevelt wasn't a native either. On the contrary, he was an Easterner who went West to become healthy and acquire some common sense.

Dakota Territory was the perfect place for his purposes.* Roosevelt worked long and hard on his ranch in the North Dakota Badlands. He learned how to ride a horse, herd cattle, work his employees, and shoot a gun.** Always on the lookout for adventure, Roosevelt once helped law officers capture a band of outlaws.

Roosevelt boasted the most wide-ranging curiosity of any president since Thomas Jefferson. Like Jefferson, he had a special interest in Nature. On the range, Roosevelt spent long hours watching ground squirrels flick their tails. He saw calves being born and wild prairie roses blooming. Apparently, Roosevelt also acquired some common sense in North Dakota because he finally went back East.

---

*Like an agricultural amoeba, Dakota Territory divided into North and South Dakota. North Dakota's nickname, *Land of the Dakotas*, provoked great fear that the state would subdivide still further, multiplying until the West was overrun with Dakotas. But winter's snows came just in time and stabilized the situation.

**These riding and shooting skills came in handy when Roosevelt led his *Roughriders* in a fearless charge up Kettle Hill in Cuba during the Spanish-American War. This conflict created a windfall for North Dakota, thus the nickname *Roughriders State* and the state flag.

Roosevelt also went up in the world — where else ca[...]
from North Dakota? — for he became our 26th President. "TR was
a President you either loved or hated. His personal motto was "Speak
softly but carry a big stick." His hobby was bullying *third world* nations.

Whether or not you agree with Roosevelt's politics, you have to
admire him for what he did for animals. He was the greatest conservationist to ever stalk the White House.

In step with his times, Roosevelt showed his appreciation for Nature by hunting big game. And he believed in biodiversity in an era
when there were no environmentalists to espouse it. TR shot moose,
elk, mountain goats, grizzly bears, black bears — just about anything
that moved. In Africa, Roosevelt's party brought down 296 big-game
animals — enough to stock a zoo — on a continent where big-game
animals are extraordinarily big, probably more than they could eat.*

Some authorities believe Roosevelt's dictum, "Speak softly but
carry a big stick," was inspired by his hunting forays. "Speak softly,"
according to this theory, was a reference to "Shhhhh," as Roosevelt
snuck up on his unsuspecting prey; the "big stick" was perhaps a reference to the gun that some Africans mistook for a third appendage.

Ever the adventurer, Roosevelt visited South America where he
journeyed down a river now named in his honor. Regrettably, Roosevelt
killed few animals on that trip; he was too sick. In fact, he lost the
health he had gone to North Dakota to find. Roosevelt might have
gone back to North Dakota to become healthy again but he was simply too busy. Besides, he had acquired common sense, remember?

To ensure a future supply of quarry, Roosevelt founded the nation's
first wildlife refuge. Pelican Island National Wildlife Refuge is located in Florida, a place Roosevelt probably thought about a lot while
he was in North Dakota.

It's no wonder Theodore Roosevelt National Park has been described as "the nation's most philosophical park." It's hard to drive

---

*Some economic analysts say the United States' outrageous national debt began
with Roosevelt's outrageous taxidermy bills.

through this scenic wonderland without thinking about bull moose and pelicans, northern pike, Lawrence Welk, healthy life-styles, and the earthworms that make North Dakota's soils (pedologists recognize several varieties) so fertile. Big sticks, that fabulous charge up Kettle Hill in Cuba...stop me, please!

Unfortunately, there will never be another Theodore Roosevelt. (He died before the development of cryogenics.) Fortunately, there will never be another North Dakota, either.

****

The preceding account, though essentially based on facts, is distorted, exaggerated. In fact, I have only the highest regards for North Dakota and North Dakotans. There is only one reason I could possibly have for criticizing my northern neighbors: Their agricultural runoff pollutes the Missouri River, the only notable natural attraction in my native South Dakota east of the Badlands.* (In *Desert Solitaire*, Edward Abbey declared that a country whose rivers are not safe to drink from is unfit to live in, adding that it is "Time then to move on, to find another country or — in the name of Jefferson — to *make* another country.")

Okay, okay, call me a hypocrite, because agriculture also rules in South Dakota, supplemented by various employment opportunities in Sioux Falls — one of the state's few bona fide cities — and ice water marketed by a drug store, which I'll discuss later. Blood is truly thicker than water — except for muddy Missouri River water — and if Louisianans and Mississippians want to complain about the agricultural pollutants we Dakotans and Montanans, Nebraskans and Kansans send their way via the nation's premier river, let them complain.

You see, I just gave you an example of Dakota humor. Where I come from — a town called Winner — people often make fun of each other in a good-natured way. In pioneer days, there was a fist fight between residents of two communities over which community would be serviced by a railroad. Residents of my town won — thus the name

---

*Tourists take note: Mitchell's Corn Palace is a *man-made* attraction.

Winner — and got the railroad, which is no longer in operation. To this day, one occasionally hears of fights in Winner, and these fights often produce a winner and a loser, just like the good ol' days.*

In the mid-West, regional ethnic humor is big, with an emphasis on Bohemians and Poles — *Bohonks* and *Pollocks* in the local lingo (*bohunks* and *polacks*, according to an editor) — and Scandinavians. Keep in mind that these jokes are frequently told by Bohemians, Poles, and Scandinavians. "You dumb Swede," passes as a greeting in South Dakota. Here's an example of a typical joke from my native habitat:

> A Bohemian and a Pollock were putting shingles on a barn when the wind blew their ladder down.
> "What are we going to do now?" cried the Pollock.
> "Don't panic," replied his companion; "you look for a way down on this side, and I'll go check out the other side."
>
> While searching for a way down, the Pollock spied his partner on the ground below.
> "How did you get down?" he asked.
> "I jumped," came the reply.
> "Jumped!? Why it's a fifty-foot fall; you never broke any bones?"
> "No, I jumped into a pile of cow manure."
> "How deep was it?"
> "Oh, it came up to about my ankles."
>
> Encouraged, the Pollock races across the barn roof and jumps into the cow manure, sinking up to his neck.
> "Ankle-deep? This is *neck*-deep, you idiot!"
> "Why, you moron," came the reply, "you must have jumped feet first!"

I realize such jokes aren't politically correct and yes, disparaging humor should be avoided where ethnic strife runs deep. But South Dakota is not like the urban wilderness in which so many Americans are lost. In fact, it's like no other state except North Dakota.

Perhaps non-Dakotans need to understand certain Dakotan institutions, namely Mt. Rushmore, Wall Drug, and the jack-a-lope, collectively monuments to South Dakotan despair, enterprise, and humor.

*The town of Redfield has recently appropriated Winner's claim to being the Pheasant Capital of South Dakota and therefore the nation. Sounds like it's time for another community brawl.

Claims that the presidents on Mt. Rushmore were sculpted by Ice Age glaciers are preposterous, as the continental glaciers never reached the Black Hills. If you could travel back in time more than 10,000 years and witness a herd of woolly mammoths plodding past Mt. Rushmore in winter however, you might *think* you were in the Ice Age — and you would be. Fossils of woolly mammoths are well represented at the nearby Hot Springs Mammoth Site, where employees can give directions to Mt. Rushmore.

Mount Rushmore National Memorial

An epidemic of urban graffiti and vandalism is spreading like a cancer throughout America's wilderness oases. The sight of toppled outhouses, vandalized picnic tables, and fluorescent wildlife is now as common as it was once shocking.

The most sensational episode of vandalism in United States history occurred in South Dakota, where an obsessive vandal equipped with enough dynamite for an army defiled an entire mountain. The damage is irreparable; merely hauling the debris away would require an enormous investment in time and money.

This vandal wasn't a total scumbag — like some taggers of the graffiti genre, he possessed crude artistic talents. Indeed, he had attempted to carve the likenesses of fellow gang members. Desperate authorities modified his "sculpture" to resemble four presidents and designated it Mount Rushmore National Memorial.

Ironically, the vandalism proved a boon — before the mountain's assailant ran amok, there were no units in South Dakota administered by the National Park Service that were worth visiting. (The Badlands is merely an example of uncontrolled erosion, while Wind Cave and Jewel Cave are underground.)

****

I write this all in jest, of course. Mt. Rushmore was in fact carved by Gutzon Borglum at the suggestion of Doane Robinson, then director of the South Dakota Historical Society. The most celebrated American sculptor of his age, Borglum was arguably a criminal however.

Borglum was carving an epic sculpture out of Georgia's Stone Mountain before he ever heard of Mt. Rushmore. Crowds flocking to the unfinished monument attracted the attention of South Dakotans. "Why not hire this guy to carve a tourist attraction out of one of our granite mountains in the Black Hills?"

Borglum liked the idea. To hell with Southern monuments; he would finish the Stone Mountain monument, then sculpt a *national* monument near the geographic center of the United States!

Upset by all the publicity South Dakotans were generating, Stone Mountain commissioners fired Borglum while he was in Washington, D.C. trying to raise money. In a rage, Borglum returned to Georgia, climbed Stone Mountain, and sent his model flying over the side. A warrant was sworn out for his arrest and Borglum fled across the North Carolina border in a midnight chase.

Bonds forged by the Civil War vanished. North Carolina militia surrounded Borglum and dared their even more southern neighbors to come and get him. Sadly, Borglum bade Stone Mountain farewell. From North Carolina, he traveled northwest to South Dakota.

Borglum's search for a sculptable monolith began in the Needles, tall rock formations that border the main highway. Many people protested his plan to deface the Black Hills. Besides, what could be carved out of a Needle, an anemic Abraham Lincoln?

So Borglum began searching for a larger and more remote formation. Remembering how British artillerymen had used the Sphinx for target practice during World War I, he wanted a high mountain. Borglum found his out-of-the-way, artillery-proof mountain. It was named for Charles Rushmore, a New York lawyer who visited the Black Hills in 1905 to inspect a client's tin mines.

The next task was to choose an appropriate subject. Many people opposed a monument honoring only George Washington and Abraham Lincoln. Everyone had their favorite hero to promote. Even today, people continue to suggest the addition of a fifth head. Susan B. Anthony is reportedly mentioned most often, other nominees including Woodrow Wilson, FDR, Eisenhower, John F. Kennedy, Dr. Martin Luther King, Clark Gable, Joe Palooka, and Mickey Mouse.

Borglum chose George Washington, Thomas Jefferson, Abraham Lincoln, and Theodore Roosevelt. Washington was selected because he is the *Father of our Country*. Jefferson best expressed Americans' beliefs in the Declaration of Independence and expanded the nation's boundaries with his Louisiana Purchase. Lincoln preserved the Union while Roosevelt fulfilled the expansionists' dream by linking the Atlantic and Pacific Oceans with the Panama Canal.

Southerners railed against "their" artist's choice of Lincoln, whom they considered a traitor. But it was the choice of Roosevelt that provoked the most ridicule. Borglum had been a leader of Roosevelt's Bull Moose Party and newspapers laughed about the resemblance between Borglum and Roosevelt.

A drive to collect money began in 1927, and President Calvin Coolidge agreed to vacation in the Black Hills. After a dedication ceremony, Borglum was lowered down Mt. Rushmore's face, where he carefully drilled four pilot holes for George Washington's head. That was the easy part: Borglum's crew of hard-rock miners would spend fourteen years, beginning in 1927, blasting away. Over 800 million pounds of stone reportedly were removed from Mount Rushmore, though it's hard to believe anyone actually weighed it.

Maintaining artistic control of a granite mountain is surprisingly difficult. Jefferson's head was started on Washington's right, but a poorly placed dynamite charge scalped him. Borglum blew the deformed head off and started again on the other side, forcing Roosevelt's head back into the rock. A hidden fault forced Roosevelt even further back, and the final carving was within ten feet of the canyon that lies behind the monument. Another ten feet of retreat might have necessitated the creation of a giant painting of Roosevelt inserted in a gaping hole.

Borglum never completed his dream. His final model depicted Washington carved to the waist, with Lincoln gripping his collar in a statesmanlike pose. (Contrary to rumors, Borglum never intended to carve North American and African wildlife at Roosevelt's feet.) Borglum died in 1941, after starting to hollow out a huge cavern in which he planned to display the record of our civilization. Borglum's son, Lincoln, completed the incomplete sculpture.

Finished or not, Mt. Rushmore is awesome. Each face is about sixty feet high from chin to forehead — twice as high as the Giza Sphinx's head. Take four sphinxes, double them in size, elevate them high above the desert, plant trees down below for shade, and you get an idea of Mt. Rushmore's grandeur. Like a series of snapshots, it pops into view time and again as your car winds its way towards the site. Standing at the foot of the mountain, one can only gawk.

I once gawked open-mouthed as a mountain goat plodded across Mt. Rushmore, like a tiny white fly. It seemed somehow appropriate, for mountain goats are not native to South Dakota, either.

In the spirit of that mountain goat, it strikes me as incongruous that a sculpted mountain in the heartland of a nation that prides itself on its diversity should depict four marvelously diverse white males. And the sculpture's diversity is exceeded by its appropriateness: One of the men portrayed — Theodore Roosevelt — actually lived for awhile in neighboring North Dakota.

Now that I think about it, perhaps Borglum's creation is appropriate. A sculpture of George Washington near the geographic center of the United States nicely balances Washington, D. C. and Washington State. Thomas Jefferson was the greatest naturalist to ever occupy the White House, and South Dakota was formerly a naturalist's paradise. Moreover, South Dakota was included in the Louisiana Purchase that Jefferson engineered. Jefferson also dispatched the explorers Lewis and Clark, who catalogued some of the most characteristic Great Plains animal species in what is now South Dakota. Without Abraham Lincoln, South Dakota might belong to the Confederacy or even to Canada. Imagine Mt. Rushmore depicting a bale of cotton or a boll weevil, or a Mountie with icicles hanging from his hat behind a team of sled dogs.

Theodore Roosevelt? The greatest conservationist to ever stalk the White House would revel in South Dakota's conservation success stories, which include the reintroduction of bison and elk to the Black Hills where they roam free as the wind within their vast enclosures.

My critics may charge that there simply are no famous South Dakotans to immortalize in stone. I refer these pseudo-historians to Joe Foss of Joe Foss Airport in Sioux Falls fame, rodeo star Casey Tibbs, the renowned poet Badger Clark, and Cheryl Ladd, who rocketed to stardom in the provocative television serial drama *Charlie's Angels*. Finally, I point with pride to renowned newscaster and caster of fishing lures Tom Brokaw, even though he now lives in Montana — much of which is pretty much like South Dakota.

In fairness, shouldn't the likenesses of some truly great women from Massachusetts and Alabama and perhaps even neighboring Nebraska be carved out of a mountain in the Black Hills? Perhaps we should rename the Black Hills the *Blank Hills* and create all sorts of surprises for visiting tourists. How about a mountain that celebrates Greg LeMond, the American who won that big bicycle race in France — the Tour de France? — in 1986, 1989, and 1990? Or let's pay tribute to members of Pennsylvania's Hershey family, of chocolate bar fame. (Will tourists wonder if the mountain is in danger of melting on hot days? Will they ask if there is a sculpture with almonds?)

I used to think it disgusting that the government of the former Soviet Union designated one of the world's great mountains "Peak Communism." Now I can't wait for them to get out their chain saws and dynamite and carve it up! Carving the likeness of President William McKinley — one American the world won't soon forget — out of North America's highest mountain will be a stupendous challenge, and will prove once again that Americans are *Number One*. It will also give Ohioans something besides tomatoes to be proud of. (McKinley was from Ohio, a state that calls tomato juice its official beverage.)

The spectacle of McKinley wearing a glacier for a cap will probably divert tourists from South Dakota. That will leave the state to revert to a cattle and ice-water economy — unless South Dakotans can come up with another really novel project for vandals. I've got dibs on Wind Cave.

Appropriate or not, Mt. Rushmore's sheer immensity is an inspiration. And it has economic value. Most of all, it gives South Dakotans something to be proud of. Mt. Rushmore's popularity probably surpasses all other South Dakotan sites administered by the National Park Service combined. And in South Dakota, there's very little besides National Park Service units to attract tourists.

The Mt. Rushmore State was recently adopted as South Dakota's official state nickname. The previous nickname, *The Sunshine State*, is shared by Florida, where sunshine is further suggested by oranges, beaches, and alligators. Feeling they couldn't compete with Florida,

70   Mount Rushmore — A Turn-off for Aliens?

South Dakota legislators dumped life-giving, crop-nourishing sunshine in favor of four deceased presidents.

When I was in the Navy, appropriately stationed on land in Canada, a friend from Rapid City told me that he and his friends used to disperse among crowds of mountain-gawkers at Mt. Rushmore. One of them would suddenly point at the mountain and exclaim something like, "Oh my God — look at that!" Some distance away, a companion would join in — "Jesus! I don't believe it!"

The excited crowd would gather round, their anxious eyes following pointing fingers, their ears pricked for verbal clues as they tried to figure out what was going on. Was an unroped climber clinging for dear life to Washington's nose? Was Jefferson being tyrannized by graffiti artists? Had Roosevelt spotted a herd of elk?

Of course, nothing was happening at all. While national parks and monuments spawn cascading waterfalls, erupting volcanoes, and photogenic wildlife, nothing ever happens at Mt. Rushmore — that's why my friend found it so funny. Mt. Rushmore is a site that compels people to see it, then move on.

Several generations ago, Mt. Rushmore might have seemed an impossibility. Might it now be possible to animate it? Perhaps the technology that put Spam on Americans' tables and Americans on the moon will filter into South Dakota. If it doesn't, perhaps South Dakotans can lure Hollywood magician Steven Spielberg to our inland empire. But first we had better ask Spielberg what sort of image he will create for Mt. Rushmore and therefore South Dakota — will his animated Mt. Rushmore be cute and sensitive like *ET*, or will it be scary, like the Tyrannosaurus in *Jurassic Park*?

In its own, quiet way, Mt. Rushmore has contributed to the sciences of anthropology and astronomy. If ancient pyramids, rock monuments, and enormous pictures gouged out of the earth were meant to attract extraterrestrials, why aren't aliens scrambling all over Mt. Rushmore? Any aliens who possess the technology to navigate interstellar space probably have monuments back home that are just as impressive as Mt. Rushmore. And they're probably animated.

THE COYOTE

South Dakota could have had a unique official nickname even before Mt. Rushmore. *The Coyote State* served as an unofficial nickname even before the coyote was designated the state animal in 1949. Unfortunately, the coyote — which, in a state where cattle are revered, was unpopular to begin with — never enhanced tourism.

My suggestion that South Dakotans carve a coyote out of a mountain fell on deaf ears. Here's another idea: Carve an *International Friendship Through Canines* memorial, reminiscent of North Dakota's International Peace Gardens. It could include a coyote, Lassie, Snoopy, a Swiss St. Bernard, and Laika, the Soviet dog who was the first animal to orbit Earth aboard *Sputnik II*. Flags representing the United States, all the republics that were carved out of the Soviet monolith, Switzerland, and the Red Cross could be sold to tourists.

Edward Abbey appreciated the coyote. In *Desert Solitaire*, he admitted that coyotes eat lambs. "Do they eat enough?" he asked like a mother concerned for her growing children. Perhaps it is the coyote's slender physique that concerned Abbey, for in another passage he suggested that domestic dogs — which, like people, are all too common — ought to be ground up and used as coyote food.

Few Americans would grind up their dogs to feed coyotes, which they hate almost as much as they hated wolves. The wolf is extinct in South Dakota, as it is in all but a few states. (It cannot be said to be extinct in Hawaii, perhaps the only state where wolves never occurred naturally. Given Hawaiians' penchant for introducing exotic animals, it's probably only a matter of time before hula dancers are serenaded by wolf howls.) Mt. Rushmore ought to include a canine lifting its leg over four presidents, to show the world what wolves and coyotes think about the U.S. government's policy toward predators, which work for a living and are useful, in stark contrast to many politicians.

I've got an idea...why don't we carve animals out of mountains across the continent! That way, people won't have to drive to national parks to see wildlife — they can view them from a distance. And stone animals are immune from extinction.

As I write this, certain people are attempting to discard South Dakota's coyote along with its sunshine. They think the bison, or "American buffalo," would make a better state animal. The bison — which already represents Wyoming, Kansas, and Oklahoma — would certainly make an appropriate ambassador of any Great Plains state. But its popularity renders it about as distinctive as the white-tailed deer, an official symbol of Nebraska and seven eastern states.

Why did they do that? The white-tailed deer wasn't discovered anywhere near Nebraska. In fact, Nebraska was originally nicknamed the *Antelope State*. That was before the state that gave us Arbor Day fenced and plowed its pronghorn-infested grasslands and enhanced its whitetail habitat by planting trees and cereal grains.

In contrast, the coyote was officially discovered in South Dakota. Spanish explorers made casual note of coyotes farther south. However, they were too intent on finding cities of gold to take much note of ungilded flora and fauna.

Lewis and Clark collected a coyote near the present tourist rest stop of Chamberlain on September 18, 1804. In his diary, Clark wrote "I killed a Prairie wolff, about the size of a gray fox bushey tail head & ears like a Wolf, Some fur Burrows in the ground and barks like a Small Dog." (Recent generations of high school students have taken to imitating Lewis and Clark's writing style. Is this welcome evidence of a growing interest in American history among our youth?)

Theodore Roosevelt championed the coyote when he debated claims that there might be several species of coyotes. Today, coyotes from Florida to Alaska bear the sole scientific name *Canis latrans*.

The National Park Service ought to designate the coyote a living national monument. While America's wilderness continues to shrink, the coyote has actually expanded its range far to the east of the Missouri River and north into Alaska. If the trend continues, coyotes may be prowling the moon before the Everglades dry up and disappear.

South Dakota alone remains the *Coyote State*. I can think of only three other carnivorous state nicknames: Michigan is the *Wolverine State*, despite the fact that that superlative member of the weasel family, with an occasional stray, apparently never lived there. Another member of the weasel family is honored by Wisconsin, but the nickname *Badger State* derives from early lead miners who spent so much time burrowing. California has been called the *Bear Flag Republic* for the now extinct California grizzly bear that graces its flag. In stark contrast to Michigan wolverines, Wisconsin badgers, and California grizzlies, South Dakota's coyote population is thriving.

Yet South Dakota's nickname is itself deceptive. The original South Dakota "coyote" was a Dakota Cavalry horse that beat an Iowa Cavalry horse in a race in 1863. One observer said the Dakota horse "ran like a kiote."

Another story has it that General Alfred Sully, watching his troops pursue Native Americans said "see the kiotes run." Thereafter, the Dakota cavalrymen were popularly called kiotes. (What if Sully had substituted an obscenity for "kiotes?" Would South Dakota now be *The #$#&@!!! State?*)

The 1949 Legislature made it official in language all Dakotans could understand: "That the coyote is hereby designated as the state animal of South Dakota." South Dakota was the first state to embrace a mammal as its state animal.

Badger Clark, South Dakota's poet laureate, commented on the coyote's soulful voice.

His notes seem to soar up to the stars and give an indescribable impression of wilderness and freedom — the voice of the Old West, the voice of a younger world. In our unhappy, overcrowded century, when the slow, steel tentacles of collectivism are gradually closing about us all and freedom is fading away, the coyote's song is as sweet — and as sad — as any music I know.*

Most of the music that comes out of the *Coyote State* is indeed sad. Local bands are often bribed not to play. Charity groups may purchase entire series of concert tickets and mercifully burn them; sometimes they burn the performers. City ordinances forbid members of marching bands to blow into their instruments. Singing in the shower is a felony. Church choirs perform in sign language. Songbirds can be hunted at any time of year, with no bag limit. The song sparrow is extinct in South Dakota

Four months after the coyote became South Dakota's state animal, Governor George T. Mickelson declared a coyote named Tootsie the state's official representative. Tootsie toured extensively with her owner, Fred Borsch, even visiting the Grand Canyon.

The *Rapid City Journal* (February 4, 1995) carried an article entitled "Coyote has marks of real South Dakotans" by Fred Borsch's niece, Jeri Borsch Fahrni, and John Fahrni.* They sum up their case for the coyote: "The value of tradition in promoting symbols for the human spirit far outweighs the value of frank commercialism. The recent film that is given much credit for promoting South Dakota is titled 'Dances with Wolves,' not 'Bison Stampede.'"

Yet Kevin Costner's epic tribute to pre-agricultural South Dakota did feature a bison stampede, filmed in South Dakota. The bison stampede in the movie *How the West Was Won* was also filmed in the *Coyote State*. Until Mt. Rushmore is animated, about the only chance we South Dakotans have of luring Hollywood to our inland empire rests on the bison's shoulders. Bison are also a greater tourist attraction than are coyotes, which are seldom visible to visitors.

We South Dakotans need to exercise the greatest caution in managing our state animal — we've blown it with most of our other symbols. The state tree and fish — Black Hills spruce and walleye — are probably outnumbered by parrots and llamas in the greater part of South Dakota. The walleye also reigns as state fish of Minnesota, which is where most South Dakotans probably go to catch walleye.

At least the Black Hills spruce and walleye connect us to the proper continent. The state bird, the ring-necked pheasant, is an Asian import, the state insect — the ubiquitous honeybee — European. All we need now are some symbols from Australia, Africa, and Madagascar. Such a roster of symbols — including Mt. Rushmore — suggests that South Dakota has nothing native worth seeing or experiencing. The State's reputation rests on the shoulders of our state animal!

*True Coincidence: I telephoned Jeri and learned that she is from Seattle, where this book was published. She says her uncle, who is nicknamed *Coyote*, used to drive around Seattle in a pickup sporting a wooden coyote in the back. My father is nicknamed *Coyote* as well. All things are connected

CRAZY HORSE

I predict that the nickname *Mt. Rushmore State* will eventually be replaced by an equine moniker. Another mountain in the Black Hills has been singled out for improvement. Promising to exceed even Mt. Rushmore in grandeur and appropriateness, this sculpture depicts the great Sioux warrior Crazy Horse mounted, appropriately, on a horse. (What if these vandals had chosen to honor Sitting Bull, or the movie *Dances With Wolves*?)

Crazy Horse's nine-story-high face is projected to be completed by the end of this decade. All four heads on nearby Mt. Rushmore could fit inside Crazy Horses' head. (It is doubtful that the sculptors will hollow his head, however.) And the horse's head is even larger. The overall sculpture will be 563 feet high and 641 feet long.

Crazy Horse Monument's educational value will be enhanced by Crazy Horse University, which will nestle at its feet. (Will South Dakota's agricultural sector trust a veterinarian with a degree from Crazy Horse University?) The Indian Museum of North America at Crazy Horse boasts an impressive collection of Native American artifacts. (When are the Sioux going to get off their butts and open up a White People Museum?)

Visitors can watch history in the making as sculptors blast away. Indeed, visitors' fees, along with contributions, finance this nonprofit, non-government enterprise. Hopefully, visitors will also help weigh the rubble that sculptors remove from the mountain.

Incidentally, *Dakota* is a Sioux word meaning "friends" or "allies". It presumably commemorates the spirit of brotherhood that existed between early pioneers and the Sioux Indians they nearly extermi- nated. Crazy Horse led the attack that wiped out "General" George A. Custer's command at the Battle of the Little Bighorn in Montana, one of the few Indian victories that Native Americans can rally around. Ironically, Crazy Horse Monument is near the town of Custer.

Like their white allies, the Sioux confused horses and canids. Be- fore they had horses, the Sioux used dogs as beasts of burden, as did many other Native Americans. This doesn't mean they chased buffalo down on "dog-back." Rather, they used dogs to carry lighter loads. The Sioux called the horse *Suktanka*, which translates as "big dog." Crazy Horse rode a big dog when he and his dog soldiers, as Sioux warriors were called, wiped out "General" Custer's command (which may have included a few *coyotes*) at the Little Bighorn — not to be confused with the Big Littlehorn — River in Montana. Got it?

Perhaps I erred in suggesting that Crazy Horse Monument is more appropriate than Mt. Rushmore. Like flags, carved mountains don't figure prominently in Native American tradition.

What the Sioux might appreciate more than a giant stone Indian that attracts even more visitors to their sacred *Paha Sapa* (Black Hills) is the return of the Black Hills, which the United States government promised them in a treaty. Of course, that was before the discovery of gold, which always overrules any treaty. And Mt. Rushmore can't be abandoned to people who might not give it the tender loving care the National Park Service does.

These are issues visitors can ponder as they hurtle down the monotonous asphalt trail that is Interstate 90 — even residents describe South Dakota as a land of miles and miles of miles and miles — wishing they could blink their eyes and find themselves in the next state. Like our pioneer forbears, they will have to tough it out until they reach the only other man-made attraction in South Dakota to rival Mt. Rushmore.

Tourist Tip: Intensely proud of their culture, South Dakotans have gone to great lengths to keep their children away from the corrupting influences of English and French. If you foolishly refer to the capital city — Pierre — as *pee.AIR*, Dakotans will likely politely look away as they try to keep from doubling up with laughter. If, on the other hand, you make even a tiny effort at pronouncing it correctly — *peer* — you will have proven your cultural sophistication. Who knows, you may even be invited in for supper!

HEEERRRRE'S WAAAALLL DRUUUUUUG!!!!

THE WATER EMPIRE

In the movie *Close Encounters of the Third Kind*, people from around the world were drawn by a vision to Devils Tower, Wyoming for a rendezvous with aliens — extraterrestrial that is, not illegal. South Dakota was the site of a similar — but genuine — phenomenon long before the movie was even conceived.

Decades ago, as though in a trance, people began to descend on the small community of Wall — its population in 1988 was 800, though it has quadrupled since then — NOT. There, Ted Hustead, a Nebraska pharmacist variously described as a Prairie Huckster and Drugstore Barnum, had built a hole-in-the-wall patent medicine store into a world-famed pharmacy. (Dorothy and Ted Hustead purchased Wall Drug in December, 1931.)

Most of the following information — including anything enclosed in quotations — is taken from the book *Free Ice Water! The Story of Wall Drug*, by Dana Close Jennings, revised by Harold & Barbara Howard, sent to me by Ted Hustead's son, Bill Hustead, President, Wall Drug Store, Inc.

Attractions

More than a mere drugstore, Wall Drug is an emporium, an institution, an industry, a fantasy-land that rivals Disneyland and Sea World in imagination if not in consumption of electricity and seawater.* The Main Street of Wall Drug's "typical western town" is made of Cheyenne River rock, the buildings that line it of a collection of native timber and old brick. There are shops with names like Calamity Jane's Jewelry Emporium, Post Card Office, Hole-In-The-Wall Book Store, Pottery and Iron Shed, The Rock Hound Shop, The Out West Clothing Store, and Big Bull Harness Shop.

*Eminently appropriate, the word emporium derives from the Greek *emporion*, a trading place or mart, which evolved from *emporia*, trade, commerce, which in turn derives from *emporos*, a traveler. Wall Drug is truly a "traveler's mart." Finally, *emporos* derives from *en*, in, and *poros*, way. I suppose this could be taken to mean that Wall Drug is *in* South Dakota, a state which is in the *way* of eastern tourists trying to reach western national parks and monuments.

Motorists can park their cars (riders can hitch their mounts to horse-headed hitching posts), then mosey on inside and enjoy Ted Hustead's animated Cowboy Orchestra, accompanied by a flea-scratching hound. An Arrowhead Room features Indian artifacts and portraits of famous chiefs. There are enough mounted animals on the walls to make Teddy Roosevelt feel right at home.*

"Souvenirs suit any taste — from the cheap junk that tourists like to haul home by the ton to objects of true ceramic art — from toys to a $175 revolver." You can buy a cheap plaster-of-paris rattlesnake ashtray or a pair of Tony Lama cowboy boots that cost over $200 — over $400 if made of alligator skin. If you purchased this book in Wall Drug's book store, then you can tell your friends back home you visited one of the best book stores in South Dakota and therefore in the Dakotas — and bought their best book to boot.

If a bellyful of ice water and free browsing leave you unsatiated, you can dine on buffalo burgers or more conventional food, complemented with a California wine, visit an old-fashioned soda fountain — the store makes its own hard and soft ice cream — then browse some more.

The Hustead's financial strategy is simple: Lure customers in with the promise of freebies and cheapies, then let them feast their eyes on the real merchandise. Wall Drug has long advertised all the coffee customers can drink for 5¢. And if 5¢ is too steep, there are options: "FREE COFFEE AND DONUTS TO HONEYMOONERS," reads another enticement. Bill Hustead comments that they also "have free coffee and donuts for veterans, hunters, honeymooners and 18-wheelers in the wintertime." An article in *Time* (August 31, 1981) quoted a honeymooning Connecticut couple as saying, "They don't try to make a lot of money off a few people, just a little money off a lot of people."

And make money they do. *USA Today* (Feb. 26, 1985) listed Wall Drug with Reyers Shoe Store (Sharon, PA), Shell Factory (North

---

*That a mounted buffalo was worn out by riders is understandable when one considers that Wall Drug now hosts an estimated 15,000 to 20,000 visitors a day during the busy months of June through August.

Fort Myers, FL), Stew Leonard's (Norwalk, CT), and Williamsburg Pottery Factory (Williamsburg, VA) in a cover story that analyzed the secrets of one-store giants.

More than a tourist gimmick, Wall Drug is more authentically South Dakotan than Mt. Rushmore. Wall Drug's walls are graced with paintings by some of the West's best known artists — including some South Dakotans. The Art Gallery Dining Room is lined with local cattle and horse brands taken from the 1889 and 1970 South Dakota brand books. Many of the brands have been in the same family for nearly a century, long after the cattle who first wore them have passed on.

For visitors who can't wait to see Mt. Rushmore, the Husteads had a replica made. Black Hills spruce, South Dakota's state tree, surrounds Mt. Rushmore. Wall Drug lies within the domain of the Great Plains' true arboreal ambassador, the cottonwood, which represents Nebraska (where Arbor Day originated), Kansas, and Wyoming.

The best known cottonwood in the Great Plains, and therefore the world, is likely the one that was swallowed by Wall Drug's cafeteria. It was growing right where the cafeteria was to be built. "We didn't dare cut it down," recalled Dorothy Hustead. "It was the first tree in Wall, planted in Ought Six, and for a long time the only tree in Wall." The cafeteria was modified to accommodate the cottonwood, which grew right through the roof — until it died and had to be removed.

Those Signs

One day in 1936, Dorothy Hustead was taking a siesta when the annoying sound of jalopies rattling by on nearby Route 16A gave her an idea. "After driving across the hot prairie, those travelers must be thirsty," she told her husband. "We've got plenty of water and ice, so why don't we put up a few signs on the highway?" She penned some doggerel, which Ted lettered on a 12-by-36-inch board: "Get a soda/ Get root beer/Turn next corner/Just as near/To Highway 16 and 14/ Free Ice Water/Wall Drug." "We hardly got back to the store from putting the sign up," recalled Ted, "before people started turning in." Because "Wall" takes up less room on a sign than "Hustead" and is also easier to remember, Hustead Drug Store became Wall Drug.

The Husteads wandered farther and farther afield in search of suitable locations for their signs, whose basic message became "FREE ICE WATER WALL DRUG, S.D." An instant hit, the signs continued to proliferate. During World War II, Leonel Jensen started erecting Wall Drug signs all over Europe. The idea caught on. Wall Drug signs boosted the morale of American troops in Korea and Vietnam.

Today, Wall Drug's walls sport "photos from all over the world showing WALL DRUG 10,728 MILES signs in front of the Taj Mahal, Eiffel Tower, Great Pyramid, 38th parallel, North Pole." More numerous in the United States, the signs reach their greatest density in South Dakota. "On I-90, fifty-four miles east of Rapid City, signs in quickening cadence announce it's Only 5 Minutes to Wall Drug, 1 Mile to Wall Drug, Wall Drug ½ mile, Wall Drug Exit.

"You turn off and a modest little sign croons in muted letters hardly three feet high, GLAD YOU MADE IT! WALL DRUG STRAIGHT AHEAD. STILL IN BUSINESS." Tourists mesmerized by the monotonous drive across the state may be shocked back to reality by a sign alerting, "YOU ARE MISSING WALL DRUG."

"I don't know how I could be so stupid," Ted Hustead fretted. "I had English signs put up in Paris." The French, who are notoriously chauvinistic about their culture, need to practice their English anyway. Signs posted in London's Underground (subway) — 5,160 miles from Wall Drug — led to a transatlantic telephone interview that was rebroadcast on BBC.

There is reportedly a Wall Drug sign — erected by Cliff Foss of Sioux Falls — in Barrow, Alaska, the United States' northernmost community and 4,500 miles from Wall Drug. (If I had known about it, I would have visited it when I was up there observing bowhead whales for the North Slope Borough Environmental Protection Office.) There's also a Wall Drug sign only 1,100 miles from the South Pole. I assume it's the one a friend from Rapid City — the one who alarmed visitors at Mt. Rushmore — advised me his uncle had put up. *Good Housekeeping* in 1951 termed the Hustead signs "the most ingenious and irresistible system of signs ever devised."

Wall Drug is advertised by over 3,000 highway signs in fifty states. "'You'll see Wall Drug signs from here to Hell,' grins the mayor [of Wall]. 'I personally put up the only Wall Drug sign in Hell. Hell, Michigan. Usta have a photo of it 'round some'rs.'"

Ever practical, "One sign near Wall is designed to provide a capacious windbreak for the rancher's cattle." But the Wall Drug sign empire is best known for its humor. Ted responded to the Big Blizzard of '49 that paralyzed the region by erecting a big sign at the city's edge reassuring customers, "STILL IN BUSINESS/WALL DRUG." A *Dakota Farmer* cartoon depicts astronauts on the moon gazing at a sign with the legend "WALL DRUG 238,857 MILES." It was printed on a post card and sold at Wall Drug.

What would be considered eyesores in most states are welcome relief to road/grasslands-weary tourists trekking across South Dakota. "Down with Lady Bird's beautification program — we want more Wall Drug signs!" wrote a visitor from Ohio.

The Wall Environment

"Set on a divide, Wall splits raindrops four ways." Surrounded by ranches and the Buffalo Gap National Grasslands, Wall gets its name from its location on the Badlands' west wall, a sharp dropoff just east of town from whence one stares down into this fantastically eroded country. (Wall Drug advertises itself as the "Gateway to the Badlands National Park," though many tourists regard it as the "Exit from Greater South Dakota.") As late as 1949, storms drove herds of cattle and horses over the precipice to perish in the gulch below, according to the authors of *Free Ice Water!*; their bones earned desperately needed money for Wall youngsters during the Depression.

"The town was established in 1907 near where the west-building and east-building Chicago & Northwestern tracks linked. Town lots were sold July 10, a gala date . . . Homesteaders' shacks promptly dotted every 160 acres and in the next few years the area had its greatest population, which began to dwindle as climatic and economic facts dictated the minimum family subsistence unit here is a thousand acres." Edward Abbey would have appreciated Wall as a place where space triumphs over Americans' preoccupation with time — Wall Drug is the only pharmacy within a 6,000-square-mile area.

Residents of this ice water boomtown still live in relative dignity. The simplicity, honesty, and comradeship nurtured by such an environment shines through in Wall Drug. "A rancher called and asked Bill about some medicine for one of his good beef cows. Bill who was extremely busy with customers answered the phone and after getting the entire story said, 'Joe, I could sell you a couple of things for that but to be honest I'd suggest you get a hold of the "vet." It sounds to me like that would be the wise thing to do.'"

This type of candor, of genuine concern about one's fellow man, has created an unusual store owned by an unusual family." This unusual family includes 250 summer employees, many of them high school and college students, and 100 winter employees.

Wall Drug receives a few bad apples, however. "Just below the cactus seeds by the praying hands is a little sign: DON'T BE ALARMED WHEN A LOUD BELL RINGS. IT JUST MEANS WE'VE CAUGHT ANOTHER SHOPLIFTER."

Wall Drug was once prepared to fend off an army of shoplifters: "Wall is the best-defended town in the world, being surrounded by fifty Minutemen missiles. Each sixty-foot long, 70,000-pound rocket can carry a nuclear warhead @ 15,000 MPH." The missile sites were manned twenty-four hours a day by personnel of the Minuteman Wing of Ellsworth Air Force Base, Rapid City. Perhaps that's why residents of other nations have been so reluctant to tamper with Wall Drug signs. The missiles have been removed from western South Dakota, however.

Wall Drug & Tourist Humor

With a clientele numbering as many as 20,000 a day, you would think that many humorous things happen at Wall Drug. Here's one recorded in *Free Ice Water!*

Dorothy sat down in a booth one day and put her hand down on the seat and thought she was bit. She'd laid her hand on a set of teeth. Figuring she hadn't heard the last of this, she tucked them into the cash register and, sure enough, in a few days she got a letter saying please send my teeth to-

A sign "out across the alley" that advertised the original ice water well, discovered by Ted Hustead in 1936, reportedly duped many tourists. Such a well would have indeed been a welcome fantasy. Ted didn't dare use the water the City of Wall collected "in a couple of stock ponds and piped" — untreated — to stores and houses. "After a year of hauling drinking water by coaster wagon, he built a thousand-gallon cistern in the back yard and hired Fred VanVleck to truck spring water from Wasta, fourteen miles west, and dump it in there."*

THE JACK-A-LOPE
(pronounced JAK.uh.lope)

The jack-a-lope is an expression of humor in the tradition of the regional ethnic jokes I wrote about earlier. In this case, the butt of the joke is not fellow South Dakotans but tourists.

Please don't get the impression that South Dakotans despise tourists. South Dakotans are generally friendly by nature. (People in rural areas — much of South Dakota can be described as an agricultural wilderness — tend to be a bit suspicious of folks who don't fit the local mold, however.) And without tourism, our economy would be at the mercy of cattle diseases. Moreover, we South Dakotans are legendary tourists ourselves; forests, mountain ranges, buildings with escalators, cultural attractions — they're all novelties to us.**

But it's hard not to feel superior when confronted with an urbanite who has never seen a cow, let alone milk one — or perform surgery on one — and who gets dizzy at the thought of several square miles of open space. And let me remind you that Easterners have been known to look down their noses at Dakotans. I've been snubbed a time or two myself in New York City and even in London (by a visiting New Yorker).

*Readers are invited to submit humorous or unusual stories or observations relating to Wall Drug to WALL DRUG TALES, Geobopological Survey, PO Box 95465, Seattle, WA 98145

**South Dakota is not as treeless as some people believe. Early pioneers planted extensive windbreaks. Trees have also been planted in most communities. Wall, for example, is no longer a one-tree town. I've also heard it said — and this may be a joke — that farmers plant trees by their mailboxes so that they can sit in the shade while waiting for their government checks to arrive.)

But the jack-a-lope is unleashed on unsuspecting tourists in a spirit of fun more than an attempt to ridicule or humiliate. Indeed, South Dakotans don't put much effort into making the trick work. Jack-a-lope stories are so preposterous they often fail to fool North Dakotans.

The jack-a-lope is a creation of South Dakota and Wyoming taxidermists; precisely when and where it debuted is probably long since forgotten. I recollect seeing dual-species jack-a-lopes, part rabbit and part deer, as a kid. I was surprised to learn that jack-a-lopes now sport wings and tail feathers from the state bird, further justifying the Latin name, *Animalculus imitatans*.

The subtlety with which the folks at Wall Drug present the jack-a-lope to visitors is recorded in *Free Ice Water!*

A card assures you solemnly that this once-rare creature is becoming more numerous with the increase of atmospheric radiation since 1960. For 25 cents you can buy an official-looking Jack-A-Lope hunting license that permits you to take them (with tranquilizer pellets in a slingshot only) between 1:00 a.m. and 4:00 a.m. above 6,000 feet the second Monday of each week provided you are a citizen of the United States or some foreign country. Only males may be taken; "...you can safely identify the male from the female as they both are antlered."

Incidentally, Wall Drug also boasts a six-foot rabbit, but it does not sport antlers.

****

In summary, South Dakota and tourists are lucky to have Wall Drug (and Mt. Rushmore), and Wall Drug is lucky to have South Dakota and tourists (and its very own Mt. Rushmore). The relationship is the envy of other states.

Tourist Tip: Don't think you can speed across South Dakota at 170 miles per hour, protected from the law by your "fuzz-buster." Law enforcement officers can simply watch you, logging your time between telephone poles. Of course, you can always drive at night, but the roads are frequently booby-trapped with cows.

BELLE FOURCHE — AMERICA'S NAVEL

At first glance, the casual visitor might think Belle Fourche is just like any other South Dakota community. But it is unlike any community in the world, for Belle Fourche is near the geographic center of the most powerful nation on Earth.

Does this seem trivial? In fact, the history of the United States has largely revolved around its ever-shifting geographic center. For a time, the center was located in the Northeast, where it was surrounded by Thirteen Colonies. As restless colonists began to push the frontier westward, the geographic center followed them.

As the center followed the setting sun across the then appropriately named mid-West, Indiana acquired the nickname *Crossroads of America*. With the annexation of Texas, the southwestern states, California, and the Oregon Territory, the Midwest became a part of the East, and the geographic center leaped across the Missouri River and came to rest near Smith Center, Kansas. (Thank God the center didn't come to rest in the middle of the Missouri — it might have been washed out to sea!)

Americans were horrified that their geographic center was located in a state known for its tornadoes. In desperation, they bought Alaska from Russia, hoping to move it to safer territory. It worked! Alaska's entrance into the Union shifted the center into Butte County, South Dakota.

(It was Abraham Lincoln's Secretary of State who purchased Alaska from Russia, making Lincoln's portrait on Mt. Rushmore eminently appropriate. Come to think of it, there might never have been a geographic center of the United States if it hadn't been for George Washington, while it was Jefferson's purchase of the Louisiana Purchase that got the center past the Missouri River. Finally, Theodore Roosevelt's cowboy days occurred not too far north of the nation's geographic center.)

When Hawaii unexpectedly joined the nation, Americans were thrown into a panic with the fear that the geographic center might come to rest on the San Andreas Fault or — most embarrassingly —

underwater along the continental shelf. But the mathematical wizards at the U.S. Coast and Geodetic Survey figured out a way to keep it in South Dakota; it was relocated a few miles further southwest at Latitude 44 minutes, 58 degrees North, Longitude 103 minutes, 46 degrees West. A marker commemorating this phenomenon is located twenty miles south, in Belle Fourche.

Kevin Wilkins, Executive Director of the Belle Fourche Chamber of Commerce, writes, "The BLM, Forest Service and City of Belle Fourche have constructed the visitors' center . . . south of the 'actual' center of the nation for the convenience of travelers, and since the center located north of Belle [Fourche] is infested with rattlesnakes." Mr. Wilkins notes that visitors like to be photographed at the nation's geographic center with their loved ones.* Its romantic reputation makes Belle Fourche the Great Plains equivalent of Niagara Falls. Moreover, the city's name, which translates "beautiful fork" in French, lends the community a cultural sophistication that is rare in America.

It is appropriate that the nation's geographic center is located in ranch country, for such an environment reflects Americans' roots and values far better than, say, an automobile production plant in Detroit City or a weapons testing range in Nevada.

Belle Fourche's proximity to Wall Drug, the Black Hills, and Wyoming's Devils Tower reinforces the region's status as a spiritual center and tourist conduit. Belle Fourchians ought to display that famous South Dakota humor by building an inland *Navel Academy.*

Not content with being the center of the United States, South Dakotans erected a monument and marker north of the state capital — Pierre, which is itself near the center of South Dakota — bolstering South Dakota's long-standing claim to be the approximate center of North America. Becoming the center of Earth will be a far greater challenge. If U.S. Coast and Geodetic Survey mathematicians can figure out a way to do it, South Dakotans will surely honor them. Perhaps we'll even carve another mountain in the Black Hills or give them their very own jack-a-lope ranch.

---

*I would like to receive photographs of readers holding this book in front of the marker commemorating the Geographic Center of the United States for possible inclusion in a sequel.

The following words are inscribed on the Center of
the Nation Plaque in Belle Fourche, South Dakota.

FOR GENERATIONS THE ACCEPTED CENTER OF THE
UNITED STATES WAS NEAR SMITH CENTER, KANSAS. THE
ADVENT OF ALASKA, BY MATHEMATICAL WIZARDRY,
SHIFTED IT INTO BUTTE COUNTY, SOUTH DAKOTA AND
WITH THE ADDITION OF HAWAII IT WAS AGAIN RELO-
CATED A FEW MILES FURTHER SOUTHWEST AT THE AP-
PROXIMATE JOINDER OF 44 DEGREES* 58 DEGREES
NORTH. WITH 103 DEGREES* 46 DEGREES WEST, WHICH
IN FACT IS LOCATED 1/10 OF A MILE DUE EAST FROM THIS
MARKER. SOUTH DAKOTA HAS LONG CLAIMED TO BE THE
APPROXIMATE CENTER OF NORTH AMERICA WITH MONU-
MENT AND MARKER NORTH OF PIERRE TO PROVE IT. THE
FLAGS OF SPAIN, FRANCE AND THE USA HAVE PRO-
CLAIMED THEIR SOVEREIGNTY OVER THIS AREA, THE
CENTER OF THE GREAT BUFFALO RANGES OF THE 19TH
CENTURY. THE GROS VENTRES, CHEYENNES, CROWS AND
SIOUX WAGED THEIR NEVER ENDING FORAYS AND WARS
HEREABOUTS. VERENDRYE, THE FIRST WHITE MAN,
PASSED CLOSE TO THIS POINT TO THE EAST IN 1743.**
THE CUSTER EXPEDITION OF 1874, ON THEIR HOMEWARD
JOURNEY, ALSO PASSED CLOSE BY AND IN 1876 GENERAL
CROOK WITH HIS STARVING HORSE MEAT EATERS, AF-
TER THE BATTLE OF SLIM BUTTES ENROUTE TO SUCCOR
IN THE BLACK HILLS, PASSED CLOSE BY. SHORTLY THERE-
AFTER TEXAS LONGHORNS REPLACED THE NOMADIC IN-
DIANS. BUTTE COUNTY, ONCE WITH 7885 SQUARE MILES
WAS WHITTLED DOWN TO 2266 SQUARE MILES IN 1908,
STILL A TENTH LARGER THAN DELAWARE. SOUTH DA-
KOTANS PROSPER UNDER THEIR STATE MOTTO: "UNDER
GOD THE PEOPLE RULE" AND ARE MIGHTY HAPPY TO
HAVE THE GREAT UNITED STATES SPREAD OUT EQUALLY
TO THE FOUR CORNERS OF THE COMPASS AROUND THIS POINT.

*Should read "minutes," rather than "degrees."

**Sieur de la Vérendrye was the first white man known to have entered what is
now South Dakota, not — as so many Dakotans believe — the first white man.

MISCELLANEOUS ATTRACTIONS

An expedition led by General George A. Custer in 1874 confirmed the century-old rumor that there is gold in the Black Hills. Today, billboards reinforce the rumor that there is gold in tourists' pockets. It almost seems one could experience the entire planet by visiting the attractions South Dakotans have dreamed up for their guests.

They begin far to the east of Wall Drug. East of the Missouri River, Mitchell advertises an Enchanted World Doll Museum and Prehistoric Indian Village ("South Dakota's only National Historic Landmark Archaeological Site open to the public"). But Mitchell's most famous attraction is the Corn Palace, originally built in 1892 to encourage settlement. Settlers were disgruntled to discover they couldn't make enough money farming to live in corn palaces of their own.

Al's Oasis is a tourist pit stop of Wall Drug proportions located on the Missouri River near where Lewis and Clark discovered the coyote. Farther west, Murdo promotes its Pioneer Auto Museum. Near the eastern edge of the Badlands is Kadoka — a Sioux word meaning "Hole in the Wall" — home of the world-famous "Outhouse Races."

Beyond Kadoka and Wall Drug is the Black Hills, where all hell breaks loose. Visit the big-as-life inhabitants of Dinosaur Park in Rapid City. Rapid also boasts the Chapel in the Hills, a replica of a famous 830-year-old *Stavkirke* (Stave Church) in Borgund, Norway. Tip your hats to Norwegians, America's first European tourists, when you visit.

Linking Rapid with Mt. Rushmore is one of the Free World's greatest monuments to Free Enterprise — "The Road to Rushmore." Along this road is Marine Life Aquarium, with porpoises, seals, and penguins. Nearby is The Maze. Its more than a mile of two-level walk ways are great practice for tourists destined for Utah's national parks and monuments. Fort Hayes is a chuckwagon supper — "dinner" to non-South Dakotans — show with an entire *Dances With Wolves* film set. Get your feet wet at Rushmore Waterslide Park. Witness such frontier skills as rattlesnake milking and alligator wrestling at Reptile Gardens. Next door, Flying T Chuckwagon offers a cowboy supper on a tin plate and a country-western show.

Bear Country USA is a drive-thru wild animal park with native South Dakotans (deer and coyotes), native South Dakotans that were exterminated but later reintroduced (bison and elk), native South Dakotans that were exterminated but which can be seen today in Bear Country USA (wolves and mountain lions), and nonnatives which roam the Black Hills today (mountain goats). True to its name, Bear Country USA also features bears.

Sitting Bull Caverns boasts unimaginably big dogtooth spar crystals — many are the size of a human fist! Thrill-seekers can check out Rapid Ride Go Kart Park. For intellectuals, there is Cosmos, which uses scientific principles to disorient visitors — "stand on the wall!"

Keystone's Parade of Presidents offers "Figures of every U.S. president . . . placed in imaginative and beautifully appointed settings." For those who like their presidents larger than life-size, Keystone offers a Rushmore Aerial Tramway. Or see Mt. Rushmore from a helicopter.

The community of Spearfish recreates one of Europe's oldest productions in its annual Passion Play. Nature buffs are passionate over Hot Springs' Mammoth Site. More than forty-seven mammoths have been discovered in this prehistoric sinkhole, where the animals apparently became trapped while seeking water. Modern tourists may be trapped in the gambling dens of Deadwood. A souvenir of the last great gold rush in the Lower 48, this former mining camp was once home to such colorful characters as Wild Bill Hickock and Calamity Jane.

Throughout the Black Hills, there are places where visitors can wash cowboy pancakes down with sasparillas, catch rainbow trout on every cast, buy postcards, play golf or tennis, jog, explore ghost towns, go rockhounding or rock climbing or dance to rock music, go four-wheeling through the tourist-saturated wilderness, or just enjoy the sunshine that lent South Dakota the former nickname *Sunshine State*.

I read the following in a 1993 edition of *Traveler Magazine*, an advertising tabloid: "Within 50 miles of Rapid City, there are two national parks, a national monument, a national memorial, a national forest, two wilderness areas, a national grassland, and two state parks." It's hard to understand how there can be two wilderness areas amidst all the communities, tourist attractions, and billboards!

Badlands National Park

If you ever get the chance to make the pilgrimage to Wall Drug and are not in too big a hurry to experience the Black Hills' cultural attractions, you might want to visit a side attraction known as the Badlands. The author of *Free Ice Water!* writes, "Work is afoot to upgrade the Badlands National Monument into a national park. The Husteads say many visitors remark, 'Yeah, we came through the Badlands but we dint see no monument.'"

Questions of this nature are a thing of the past, as the Badlands have indeed been designated a national park. On the other hand, is it possible that visitors to this barren environment might inquire, "Where is the park?" Perhaps it should just be called the National Badlands.

The White River Badlands, as they are also known, are inhabited by such wild creatures as bison and pronghorns.* But they are best known for their bones of mammals that lived during the Oligocene Epoch, some 30 million years after dinosaurs ended their reign of terror.

If you are not into animals, living or extinct, you still might enjoy Badlands National Park merely for its scenic beauty. A word of caution: Don't attempt backpacking in the Badlands in winter. My first attempt was also my last.

No, it wasn't cold. All the cold-weather gear I lugged around was dead weight. The problem was that it was too warm. With what little snow there was melting a few days before Christmas, I clumped around helplessly for the better part of a day with heavy lumps of clay sticking to my boots. If any Park Rangers had seen me, they might have mistaken me for a tourist. I finally gave up and hitched a ride out of the Badlands with a rural mail carrier who was passing through.

*Theodore Roosevelt National Park is located in the Little Missouri Badlands.

Tourist Tip: When driving across South Dakota, don't take a compass bearing on a distant butte, tree, or heavenly body and drive mindlessly towards it. The state's roads are treacherous — some of them have curves.

****

Scandinavians, Hispanics, Indians, Native Americans, tourists, farmers — we all share certain bonds. We all breathe air and drink water — and love ice water on hot days — and laugh at government bureaucracy and jack-a-lopes.

Soil is another item that unites humanity. I earlier poked fun at North Dakota's state motto, "Strength From the Soil." In truth, it's one of the nation's most powerful mottoes. Few things are so important yet so little appreciated as soils. *APRES BONDIE CEST LA TER,* proclaims Dominica's coat of arms in the local patois — "After the Good Lord, We Love the Earth." South Dakota's state soil — yes, it recognizes such a designation, as do a growing number of states — may in fact be its premier symbol.

The next time you trek across South Dakota, pull over anywhere between the Missouri River and Wall Drug, walk a hundred yards from the highway, take off your shoes and socks, and press your bare feet into the fertile soil. (Who knows, you may have eaten food made from wheat, corn, or beef harvested from this very field or pasture.) Turn your back to the highway, with its stream of vacationing automatons racing mindlessly towards a horizon that would be considered a natural phenomenon in many states. Read the next paragraph, then look in a direction that offers the fewest clues to human enterprise. Savor the solitude, serenity, and space as you ponder, so near America's geographic center but — more importantly — engulfed in a singular, even spiritual realm where the wilderness that was so quickly plowed under seems poised to reclaim the land.

I earlier admitted that the ethnic jokes with which some Dakotans tease each other might be inappropriate in a large city. Is it possible that the wounds that separate residents of America's metropolises will someday heal to the point that people can engage in such put-downs and exchange smiles rather than small arms fire? I witnessed evidence of this potential in a kindergarten class I taught a few years ago. A black boy hugged an Asian colleague and affectionately called him "nigger," transforming one of the dirtiest words in the American dialect into a term of endearment. Deep inside, we're all Bohemians.

****

Yes, I wrote a lot about South Dakota. For readers who do not plan on visiting South Dakota during this lifetime — or any other lifetime — I beg your pardon. Readers who plan on driving across South Dakota enroute to the Black Hills, Yellowstone National Park, or even Craters of the Moon National Monument in Idaho, however, will find this section an entertaining and educational diversion during their seven-hour trip (at the recommended — though seldom observed — speed of 55 mph) across the *Mt. Rushmore/Coyote/Crazy Horse/* (formerly) *Sunshine State*. Be sure to stop at Wall Drug for some of their home-brewed ice water. And don't forget to see Mt. Rushmore while you're there.

P.S. After writing all that stuff about the coyote, I learned that its position as South Dakota's state animal remains intact; the buffalo faction, Black Hills residents who apparently wanted to promote the bison for its tourist-appeal, lost — this time.

BONUS PICTURE SECTION!
Images of the Dakotas!

Theodore Roosevelt's big game armada and herds of prong-horn that survived his depredations are but the beginning of a photo-illustration essay that will convince you that the Dakotas deserve to be — and perhaps already are — America's largest national park.

(Above) Theodore Roosevelt commandeered the "Great White Fleet" so that he could hunt big game from sea, then began digging the Panama Canal so that he could also hunt in the Pacific. Outraged taxpayers forced Congress to delegate people to help Roosevelt dig, and the Panama Canal was opened to ships in 1914, sixty-seven years ahead of schedule. Fearful for their cows, ranchers asked their old friend not to bring the Great White Fleet up the Missouri River to Dakota Territory. A true cowboy, Roosevelt obliged.

(Opposite Page) Despite the name similarities, the pronghorn is related to neither the jack-a-lope nor Old World antelope. The scientific name *Antilocapra americana* is a reminder that the pronghorn evolved in North America, unlike the jack-a-lope, which emigrated from China. Although Buffalo Bill and Theodore Roosevelt nearly exterminated bison, elk, and grizzly bears, the speedy pronghorn still roams much of the West.

Despite all the one-dollar bills, Washington State flags, and monuments you might have seen, historians tell us that George Washington was capable of smiling — and he had good reason to. If it weren't for George Washington there would be no United States and thus no National Park Service, USDA Forest Service, U.S. Fish and Wildlife Service, Bureau of Land Management, or geographic center of the United States. The National Park Service administers the Washington Monument in Washington, D.C., South Dakota's Mt. Rushmore National Memorial, and some wilderness areas in the State of Washington. Have you ever heard someone say they are a "poet and don't even know it?" Substitute "conservationist" for "poet" and apply it to George Washington: He introduced the first Chinese ring-necked pheasants — South Dakota's state bird — into America. Two centuries later, the spectacular bird has rescued the northern Great Plains jack-a-lope from extinction (see page 217). Every summer, desperate tourists frantically exchange countless thousands of one-dollar bills bearing Washington's likeness for the gasoline they need to escape from South Dakota.

Tourist Tip: George Washington is furthest to the left on Mt. Rushmore. (He is furthest to the *right* if you are viewing the back of the mountain.)

Abraham Lincoln's most highly acclaimed biographer, Carl Sandburg, wrote a highly acclaimed series about Lincoln. A son of the American frontier, Lincoln helped preserve Yosemite before Yellowstone National Park was established. Americans can also thank Lincoln for one of our most elegant state flags, for it was his Secretary of State who purchased Alaska from Russia, just two years after Lincoln's assassination. This gave Americans a wilderness playground — with the oil reserves that will keep Prince William Sound's wilderness beaches from squeaking into the next millennium — and moved the nation's geographic center closer to its present site near Belle Fourche, South Dakota in one fell swoop. Lincoln's untimely assassination had surprising repercussions in Utah. National Park Service-administered units that honor Lincoln include Mt. Rushmore National Memorial, Gettysburg National Military Park, Ford's Theater National Historic Site, and the Lincoln Monument. The latter portrays Lincoln sitting in one of his favorite pieces of furniture — a chair. Lincoln's love for books makes him an inspiration for children lost in America's public education wilderness.

Tourist Tip: Abraham Lincoln is furthest to the right on Mt. Rushmore. (He is furthest to the *left* if you are viewing the back of the mountain.)

Thomas Jefferson's exploits as a warrior or a commander-in-chief don't begin to match those of his companions on Mt. Rushmore. Nor did he survey any swamps or establish any national parks, monuments, or wildlife refuges. Yet he was the most accomplished presidential naturalist. Virginia's official state fossil, the scallop *Chesapectens jeffersonius*, is named for Jefferson, as is the ground sloth *Megalonyx jeffersonius* which was proposed for adoption as Washington State's official fossil. A sworn enemy of tyrants, Jefferson once sent a really big stuffed moose to an European intellectual snob who had snubbed North American wildlife as "inferior." Jefferson also engineered the purchase of the Louisiana Territory, jerking the nation's geographic center far to the west, then dispatched Lewis and Clark to explore the nation's new backyard. This milestone in American history is commemorated by the Jefferson National Expansion Memorial in St. Louis, Missouri. Disgruntled residents of northern California and southern Oregon have talked of forming a new state called Jefferson.

Tourist Tip: Thomas Jefferson is second from left on Mt. Rushmore. (He is *third* from the left if you are viewing the back of the mountain.)

America's favorite bully, Theodore Roosevelt (alias TR) rivaled Buffalo Bill as an exterminator of big game, yet charmed Americans by sparing the life of a black bear cub — the first "Teddy bear." His rough-and-tumble life-style left TR's hats almost invariably smashed. TR established the nation's first national wildlife refuge — Pelican Island, Florida — and led a famous charge up a hill on another island in the Caribbean. By odd coincidence, the National Park Service administers a Theodore Roosevelt Island in the Potomac River. Any wildlife that once lived there has long since been blown away. TR was the only famous American to ever live in North Dakota, aside from the *Dakota Music Machine*, Lawrence Welk. And TR championed South Dakota's most sacred icon by arguing that there is only one coyote. One can hardly gaze at Mt. Rushmore without thinking about bull moose, Roosevelt elk, pelicans, North Dakota's inspirational state flag — a souvenir of Roosevelt's adventure in Cuba — big sticks, rowdy cowboy parties, outrageous taxidermy bills — stop me, please!

Tourist Tip: Theodore Roosevelt is second from right on Mt. Rushmore. (He is second from *left* if you are viewing the back of the mountain.)

Crazy Horse's Sioux name, *Tashunca-Uitco*, more accurately translates as "Wild" or "Unbroken Horse." We don't know exactly what he looked like, because he was never photographed. If Crazy Horse had been photographed, he probably would have appeared sullen like most great Indian chiefs of his day who were captured on film. Crazy Horse led the attack that annihilated (ex-) General George Armstrong Custer at the Battle of the Little Bighorn in Montana. The great Sioux warrior might have greeted the European interlopers who invaded his homeland with open arms if he could have foreseen the honors they would later heap upon him and his people. These include five neighboring states whose names derive from the Sioux language (North Dakota, South Dakota, Minnesota, Nebraska, and Kansas); more amusement parks than one could visit in a tourist season and an enormous sculpture of Crazy Horse on horseback — all in the Black Hills, the Sioux's sacred *Paha Sapa*; some of the nation's most scenic reservations; such idioms as "Indian giver;" and an endless array of books that disparage the way white people treated Native Americans. Washington, Jefferson, Roosevelt, and Lincoln are in one way or another commemorated by the state flags of Washington, Virginia, North Dakota, and Alaska. But flags, like sculpted mountains, were not a part of traditional Native American culture. If Crazy Horse had a favorite flag, it was probably the flag of surrender Custer wished he had brought along to the Little Bighorn in Montana.

Tourist Tip: Crazy Horse is the only person depicted on Crazy Horse Monument. The animal is a horse.

Agricultural wilderness or urban sprawl? South Dakota boasts both.
(Top) South Dakota is sometimes called the *Coyote State*, even though coyotes now rank behind beef, cereal crops, ice water, and tourists as the state's most valuable export. (Bottom) It's an eerie feeling sipping ice water in Wall Drug, surrounded by the ghosts of Minutemen missiles and more wild animals than you will probably see in whatever national park it is you're headed towards, not more than 100 miles from the geographic center of the United States and right next to the third worst example of erosion in the United States — next to Oklahoma, which largely blew away during the Dustbowl, and the Grand Canyon — and with a replica of Mt. Rushmore to boot.

(Above) Although North Dakota has fewer human residents than most national parks, its wildlife still manage to come into contact with humans. North Dakota's unofficial state animal, this pathetic Richardson's ground squirrel, alias *flickertail*, exhibits its craving for cigarettes. The rodent on the opposite page is a thirteen-lined ground squirrel, the dominant ground squirrel species in South Dakota. It recalls the thirteen colonies whose residents, after growing tired of passing back and forth through the Dakotas between the cultured East and the scenic West, reluctantly annexed Dakota Territory so that they could build a highway across it.

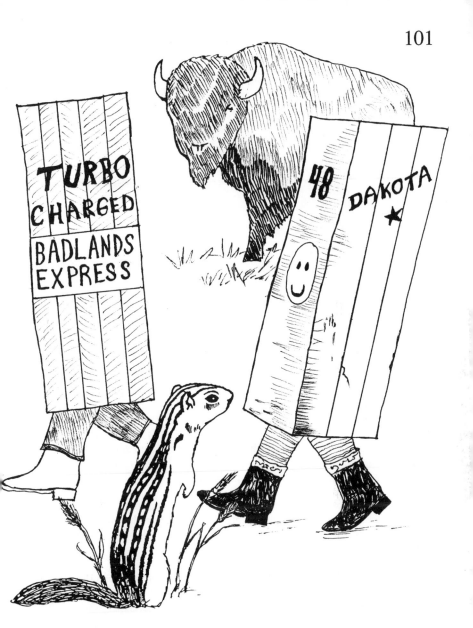

(Above) Kadoka's outhouse races are eerily reminiscent of the buffalo stampedes — filmed in South Dakota — that enliven the movies *How the West Was Won* and *Dances With Wolves*. The races recall the era when pioneers were forced to carry outhouses across the Great Plains to the *Promised Land*, a term loosely applied to anything beyond, above, or beneath the Dakotas. Outhouses furnished protection from the elements and served as vantage points for scouting game. Sadly, many outhouses were left behind as grave markers. Since the outhouses also functioned as living quarters, occupants were ironically forced to search elsewhere for toilet facilities.

(Above) His accomplishments as an adventurer are beyond dispute, and he was Norwegian and therefore a descendant of America's first European tourists. Still, anthropologists have questioned sailor/rafter extraordinaire Thor Heyerdahl's scientific methods. If he had seen this sign, might Heyerdahl have concluded that Easter Island was discovered and settled by South Dakotans? The similarity between the island's famous monoliths and Mt. Rushmore does seem more than coincidental.

(Opposite page, top) Who says evolution means progress? Millions of years ago, diverse and spectacular plants and animals flourished here. Today, Badlands National Park preserves a barren, uninhabited, prehistoric landscape similar to the surrounding state of South Dakota.

(Opposite page, bottom) Although the Black Hills spruce is the state tree, most South Dakotans are more familiar with the telephone pole, evidence that even Dakotans can't escape the Information Age. Most South Dakotans have learned that telephone poles cannot be tapped for maple syrup, but poles are still chopped down for use as Christmas trees. This South Dakotan family is attempting to tap into power lines in hopes of hearing news from the outside world that is rumored to lurk beyond the grasslands. Many hundreds of South Dakotans die from such practices each year. Holed up in the capital city of Pierre — say *peer*; incorrectly pronounced *pee.AIR* by the French — the State Government each spring launches expeditions into the Outback which bring news of the telephone to agricultural aboriginals. Known for their neighborliness, South Dakotans eagerly share this technology with North Dakotans.

Bryce Canyon National Park is one of several parks and monuments in the western United States that showcase irrational landforms. Without such freaks of Nature, much of Utah would be as bleak as the Dakotas.

THE WEST

Even the Landforms are Irrational

Eastern national parks and monuments preserve mere meadows compared to the vast patches of mountains, forests, grasslands, and deserts out West. The *real* national parks and monuments begin west of the Missouri River, on beyond the Dakotas.

Some Easterners will point out that their states boast Park Ranger-patrolled Revolutionary and Civil War battle sites. These units, they may argue, represent the nation's cultural heritage.

Like Edward Abbey — author of the classic *Desert Solitaire* — I prefer civilization and the pinnacle of American civilization lies in the uncivilized West. National parks are about unfettered animals and trees, pristine mountains and rivers. In my opinion, the only culture that matters consists of rock petroglyphs carved by ancient Native Americans, humorous quips, questions, and anecdotes related by ancient rangers, and songs sung around campfires which devour ancient trees.

You want history? Fossil trilobites in Nevada and California and algal stromatolites found in the Rocky Mountains *predate* history. These life-forms lived as much as a billion years before there was a Caribbean for Columbus to get lost in. (Stromatolites and trilobites are also found east of the Missouri River, but one is likely to be drenched with acid rain while searching for them.)

Do you prefer your wildlife alive? The West hosts spectacular grizzlies, mountain lions, wolves, bison, moose, elk, pronghorns, bighorn sheep, mountain goats, California condors, and California redwoods. The only big animals one is likely to see in the East are black bears and the moose that inhabit the northern frontier bordering Canada.

Life-forms that evolved before brains were invented and their descendants are but icing on the cake. The West has a near monopoly on wilderness, primarily because it is far from the civilized East.

Besides big animals and wilderness the West has scenery. Can you imagine a ski resort rivaling Aspen or Sun Valley in Florida? How about a Grand Canyon in Iowa, or a California coast in Ohio? Have you ever seen an Ansel Adams photograph taken east of the Missouri? Have you ever seen Ansel Adams east of the Missouri?

As if wilderness, wildlife — fossilized or not — and spectacular scenery aren't enough, the West is a geological carnival. Irrational landforms are particularly abundant in Utah, where they are preserved for posterity in such national parks and monuments as Arches, Bryce Canyon, Cedar Breaks, Canyonlands, Capitol Reef, Natural Bridges, Rainbow Bridge, and Zion. Far from being ashamed of these freaks of Nature, the folks at Bryce Canyon National Park chose *Hoodoo* — "a pinnacle, or odd-shaped rock left standing by the forces of erosion" — as a name for the Park's newspaper.

Writing about rocks and freaks of Nature brings me back to fossils, for the West's most spectacular treasures may well lie underground. Millions of fossils await discovery in the East. (There are up to one million in Florida alone, subsisting on social security.) But they are mostly unimaginably ancient marine invertebrates — things like trilobites, brachiopods, and crinoids. Such *animaloids* are not without scientific merit, but it's hard to get tourists excited over spineless, brainless creatures that crawled around in the mud several hundred million years ago, let alone algae that became petrified where it grew.

DINOSAURS. That's what excites people. Would *Jurassic Park* have been a commercial success if its creators had animated trilobites? Imagine the terror when a brachiopod clamps shut on a careless paleontologist's finger! What ten-year-old would go trick or treating as a crinoid?

Eons of erosion erased evidence of dinosaurs in Appalachia and the Midwest, while dinosaur fossils along the Atlantic and Gulf coastal plains lie buried under younger sediments. North America's dinosaur mother-lode lies on the far side of the Missouri River, where fossils from the Mesozoic Era — the Age of Dinosaurs — were alternately protected by blankets of sediments shed from the Rocky Mountains and exposed by erosion, particularly in "badlands." The most exciting dinosaur fossils in the East are footprints.

The Connecticut Valley's first dinosaur track was discovered in Massachusetts in 1802, shortly before Lewis and Clark departed on their epic journey across the continent. An amateur paleontologist, Thomas Jefferson urged his designated tourists to be on the lookout for *Megalonyx* ("giant claw") and "mammoths" (mastodons), whose bones had been discovered in Kentucky. *Megalonyx* was the name Jefferson gave to a claw which he believed at first to represent a giant cat. It was later determined to represent a giant ground sloth.

The explorers found no elephants, giant cats, sloths, or politicians lurking beyond the frontier. But Lewis and Clark may have been the first whites to discover a dinosaur fossil in the American West. Their unidentified discovery was made in Montana, where the Hell Creek Formation, known today for its fossils of such Cretaceous dinosaurs as *Tyrannosaurus rex* and *Triceratops*, crops out. (If Lewis and Clark had discovered *Tyrannosaurus rex* it would certainly bear a different name today, as Jefferson had a passionate hatred of tyranny.)

Other western dinosaurs, including a Montana hadrosaur, were discovered even before New Jersey's *Hadrosaurus foulkii* (discussed on page 49). In his book *Digging Dinosaurs*, paleontologist John Horner notes that some of the first dinosaur fossils found in North America were a collection of teeth — including one from a hadrosaur — found by paleontologist Ferdinand Hayden in Montana's Judith River formation in 1854. This was twenty-two years before Custer was defeated by Crazy Horse in Montana. How could a lone paleontologist survive where an ex-Civil War general couldn't?

Horner notes that the Indians considered Hayden "insane and therefore holy." Still, Horner notes that Hayden didnt collect fossils with blissful abandon:

> They had a name for him, and I think if you imagine a paleontologist caught unwittingly in some sort of skirmish and trying to get that last hadrosaur tooth pried out of the mudstone before he gets a bullet or an arrow in him, the name acquires its proper resonance: he was called "the man who picks up stones while running."

Paleontologists converged on the West after the Civil War. Some of the most spectacular discoveries were made near where Wyoming, Colorado, and Utah meet. Out of the earth came teeth and bones of behemoths from an alien world. Their discoverers saddled them with impossible names which would nevertheless become household words: *Brontosaurus* (properly known as *Apatosaurus*), *Stegosaurus*, *Triceratops*, *Allosaurus*, *Tyrannosaurus*. Lacking even a plaque at its discovery site, Foulke's hadrosaur was forgotten.

Dinosaurs continue to fascinate Americans as paleontologists — after taking notes from Phil, Oprah, and their ilk — probe ever deeper into their ecological relationships, physiology, sex lives, and intelligence. (One of my geology professors at Western Washington University used to joke that an extra brain between their hind legs — actually an enlarged nerve mass — helped dinosaurs get around corners.)

That Westerners are proud of their wilderness, wildlife, fossils, and freedom is evidenced by their state flags. None stand taller than Texas' Lone Star banner, while those of Alaska, New Mexico, and Arizona are unsurpassed for elegance. Flags representing Oklahoma, Wyoming, Colorado, and California also ride tall in the saddle.

The proudest Americans ought to be school teachers from Texas, Oklahoma, New Mexico, Arizona, Wyoming, Colorado, California, and Alaska who work in the summer as rangers. Is it any coincidence that Wyoming and California boast the nation's first national parks and monuments, Alaska its largest and wildest?

THE GREAT PLAINS
They're Plainly Great!

The Great Plains — a vast domain of semiarid grasslands that includes the Dakotas — is a study in irony. It ranks among the least densely populated regions in the United States, yet boasts a poverty of national parks, monuments, cultural sites, and forests. Why?

The lack of national forests and cultural sites is easily explained: There are few trees and only agri-culture here. To understand why there are so few national parks or monuments, one must consider topography. There is none. This lack of topography made it easy for settlers to exterminate wildlife, plow the land, and erect fences.

Today, this agricultural wilderness is exacerbating the growing pains of America's cities and suburbs. Populations are declining in many portions of the already under-inhabited Great Plains as young people emigrate to greener pastures — or even to urban areas — or as families visit national parks and cultural attractions in other states and can't find their way back home. The uncertainties of agribusiness are trivial compared to the crisis now facing America's Great Plains farms and ranches — a dearth of young inheritors.

In a sense, all Americans are inheriting farms and ranches in the Great Plains. Agricultural aborigines often complain about their tax-dollars being used to support welfare queens in Los Angeles. Ironically, coastal welfare queens — whose ranks likely include Great Plains emigrants — pay taxes that are plowed into farm subsidies.

There are three solutions to this problem: 1) Resettle America's urban homeless in the Great Plains, where they can sleep anywhere they want and perhaps find work as farm- and ranch-hands; 2) Convert the Great Plains into the largest shopping mall in the galaxy; or 3) Designate the Great Plains a national park, replacing subsidized farms with self-supporting herds of bison, pronghorns, and jack-a-lopes.

My last suggestion is eerily similar to one proposed by Frank and Deborah Popper, described as "an academic couple from suburban New Jersey" in Anne Matthews' book, *Where the Buffalo Roam*. Noting that ". . . much of the Great Plains is in the process of reverting to frontier conditions only a century after the frontier was declared officially closed," the Hoppers proposed that a quarter of the Plains — 139,000 square miles in ten states — be set aside as a massive ecological reserve which they call the Buffalo Commons.

This proposal infuriated many Great Plains residents. Others humbly asked whether they were worthy of such a designation. "Tell the Poppers that America's Great Plains don't equal the Sahara," said Kansas Governor Mike Hayden. That's true, the Great Plains lack the Sahara's scenic wonders and epic archaeological sites. But the Poppers were talking about an ecological reserve, not a national park.

In fact, Great Plains sod covers *Tyrannosaurus rex* skeletons more exciting than any Egyptian mummy, while Montana boasts a historic site that reminds us of a conflict more recent than the Civil War. And like the Civil War, it is not forgotten.

****

A less than outstanding U.S. Military Academy graduate, George Armstrong Custer needed only a battlefield to prove his worth. He found many of them as a Union soldier during the Civil War, when he distinguished himself by capturing the first Confederate battle flag and receiving General Robert E. Lee's flag of truce at Appamattox Courthouse. Custer's courage, initiative, and flair earned him an appointment as brigadier general of volunteers at age 23, and he subsequently enjoyed a string of successes at Gettysburg and other battle sites. Custer's daring, almost reckless leadership resulted in his closing the war with the rank of major general and lent him an aura that made him the most photographed man of the 19th century.

After the Civil War, Custer headed west, where Native Americans impeded America's Manifest Destiny. (Though demoted to Lieutenant-Colonel after the Civil War, Custer was and is popularly referred to as "General.") Thanks largely to their superior horsemanship and the open terrain, the Plains tribes were a greater obstacle than most.

June 22, 1876 found Custer leading his regiment from a base camp on the Yellowstone River, Montana enroute to a suspected Indian encampment. These Indians were and are commonly described as "hostile." To avoid persecution at the hands of the *politically-correct-police*, I will apply the term "hostile" to all parties.

It was hoped that *hostile* Custer could coordinate his attack with another *hostile* command marching south along the Little Bighorn River. But a large *hostile* Indian village was discovered on the Little Bighorn early on June 25. Fearing discovery, Custer attacked at once, splitting his regiment of about 650 men into four detachments.

The village counted some 1,500 residents — and they did not include women and children. Custer was driven by Sioux and Northern Cheyenne warriors led by Crazy Horse into broken ground that hampered his cavalry. Forced to fight on foot, his force of 225 soldiers was annihilated in little more than an hour; only a *hostile* horse named Comanche survived. The remainder of the 7th cavalry took up a defensive position on the bluffs above the Little Bighorn, where it was relieved by another *hostile* column a couple days later.

This battle is called the Custer massacre, Custer's last stand, a great Sioux victory, or — in a spirit of compromise — the Battle of the Little Bighorn. Compared to the carnage of the then recent Civil War the battle was insignificant. Yet Americans were stunned. Indignant whites had their revenge at Wounded Knee, South Dakota, where *hostile* unarmed Indians, young and old, were gunned down in winter's cold. Even today, some people see Custer as a hero. Native Americans have a different perspective: "Custer died for your sins."

Like some Civil War engagements, the Battle of the Little Bighorn is regularly reenacted. In the May/June 1995 issue of *Montana Magazine*, Billings (Montana) writer-historian Robert Kelleher, Jr. analyzes the battle's mystique in an article entitled "Rematch at Little Big Horn."

Why does the Little Big Horn Battle so fascinate the American psyche? Objectively, the loss of 225 men is minor compared to casualty rates in other conflicts. In contrast, the U.S. Army lost that many men in the first 30 seconds on Omaha Beach. The answer to the Custer fascination is that the defeat of five cavalry companies atop a desolate Montana hill gave Americans a triple shock. First, the fallen commander of the Seventh Cavalry, General George Armstrong Custer, was a hero of the American Civil War. Children in the 1870s collected photos of Civil War heroes (called *cartes de visite*) the way children today collect baseball cards. Custer was a favorite.

Second, the battle took place on June 25, 1876, just nine days before the July 4 national centennial. Word of the defeat filtered to cities in the East just as the American public began celebrating the 100th anniversary of the Declaration of Independence. Finally, the defeat of U.S. troops at the hands of the Sioux and Cheyenne jolted American sensibilities because nearly all believed that 'savage' Indians were no match for the United States military. (In fact, most of Custer's troops had never been in combat, nor had they fired more than a few dozen rounds in training. Most Indian warriors had been fighting other Indians since childhood.)

The spell the Custer massacre/Crazy Horse victory still holds over Americans was driven home one day on a research vessel in Alaska. I was exchanging banter with the ship's captain when the conversation turned to the Battle of the Little Bighorn. I commented that it seemed appropriate that the then current superintendent was a Native American woman. My companion suddenly became *hostile*. Exploding in anger, he started *bellering* about Indians, justice, and fishing rights; he said he had suffered financially because of "all this Indian crap." He was referring, I think, to a court case in the State of Washington which restored aboriginal fishing rights to Native Americans.

Students of history know that the Plains Indian War was not about fish so much as bison vs cattle, grasslands vs agriculture, and genocide vs freedom. Whites did not recognize Great Plains residents as people with rights, partly because Native Americans did not recognize national boundaries. Nor did they fly national flags. They were merely primitive tribes standing in the way of progress. "They weren't doing anything with the land, anyway," I've heard many people say.

Since all things are connected, perhaps there is some connection between the Battle of the Little Bighorn and the North Pacific salmon industry. I suppose one might even draw some sort of analogy between the story of the Sioux and Madagascar's environmental woes. At any rate, the battle continues to stir passions.

The site was established as a national cemetery in 1879, proclaimed National Cemetery of Custer's Battlefield Reservation in 1886. Transferred from the War Department, it became Custer Battlefield National Monument in 1946. In 1991, it was finally renamed **Little Bighorn Battlefield National Monument**. A *hostile* correspondent employed at a unit east of the Missouri River offers this item.

> My other all time favorite story happened in the summer of 1984 at Custer Battlefield National Monument. This was before the name of the park was changed to Little Bighorn Battlefield National Monument. I had finished what I had felt was one of my best delivered Battle Talks, an introductory overview of the battle for the general public. During the program I had described that it appeared to the burial parties that once reaching the highest ground available, some of the soldiers shot their horses to provide cover from Indian bullets fired at them from lower ground. After the program, one visitor asked me how the soldiers got their horses inside the fence. The National Park

Service had erected an iron fence around the Last Stand Site to prevent excessive pedestrian traffic from killing all the native prairie grass.

How ironic that a battlefield commemorating one of the few glitches in a campaign of ethnic cleansing now protects native prairie grasses!

Another Park Ranger recalls a visitor who wandered into the Visitor Center and asked, "Did General Custer die here or at the Alamo?" He says rangers "scattered like dandelion seeds before they embarrassed themselves (by laughing)." One ranger, who was a drama student, maintained his composure and explained, "I think maybe you might be thinking about Davy Crockett. He was killed at the Alamo."

But does Custer, like Elvis Presley, live on? Some Native Americans believe Custer has been reincarnated in the guise of Steve Alexander. "Physically he bears an uncanny resemblance to the general," comments Kelleher. Alexander is from Jackson, Michigan, near Custer's home town of Monroe. His interest in the Old West was sparked by a grandfather who homesteaded near Glasgow, Montana. Alexander tours North America portraying Custer in Civil War and Indian War reenactments.

According to Alexander, Custer may have been given a bum rap. Kelleher asked Alexander, "What is the most common misconception about Custer? 'That he was an Indian hater. I don't think he was.' Alexander pointed out Custer hunted buffalo with Indians while dressed in buckskins and hair feathers." Alexander describes Custer as "an Indian wanna-be," yet he was very patriotic and is credited with starting the tradition of standing for the "Star Spangled Banner" before it was adopted as our national anthem.

Alexander finally describes Custer as creating a "Hollywood image," noting his "flare for drama" and his desire to "make himself larger than life." Ironically, all of Custer's wishes and passions — war, patriotism, fame — were consummated by a "primitive savage," a fellow warrior and enigma who was a mystery even to the Sioux and who was never photographed. In return, Custer gave the Sioux their sole consolation for their lost Great Plains. Far from a tragedy, the Battle of the Little Bighorn was a spectacular success for both sides. Rather than viewing the event with divisive bitterness, Americans ought to embrace it as a multicultural collaboration.

Robert Kelleher Jr. photographed Steve Alexander — declared the "foremost Custer living authority" by the Ohio Senate in 1990 — and Kathy Justus, who plays Custer's wife, on the set used in the ABC mini-series *Son of the Morning Star* and *Return to Lonesome Dove*. The house is a reproduction of the Custer home at Fort Abraham Lincoln, Dakota Territory.

****

Bent's Old Fort National Historic Site, Colorado, is something Custer should have taken with him to the Little Bighorn. An Anglo-American outpost on the Southern Plains, Bent's Old Fort was an Indian trading center and a bastion of Eastern civilization on the Santa Fe Trail. The present fort is a reconstruction. A Park Ranger currently attached to a site east of the Missouri River says one of his most memorable questions was asked at Bent's Old Fort, presumably the *new* Bent's Old Fort rather than the original.

> One day in the spring of 1989 at Bent's Old Fort in Southeast Colorado, I was explaining the history of the fort to a handful of visitors. I explained in some detail that the fort was established as a private trading post and not a military installation. Cheyenne and Arapaho Indians traded . . . buffalo hides for manufactured goods from the United States. Mexican traders from Santa Fe exchanged blankets and silver for American made products. After my talk, one lady asked me which wall of the fort the Indians most frequently attacked with their scaling ladders. This illustrates the powerful and often negative and inaccurate images of history that Hollywood has inflicted on the public.

ROCKY MOUNTAIN HIGH

It Begins In Nebraska

Some of America's most magnificent national parks nestle in the Rocky Mountains. These wonderlands include Montana's Glacier National Park, Wyoming's Yellowstone National Park, and the quintessential Rocky Mountain national park, Colorado's Rocky Mountain National Park. All three states commemorate their alpine heritage on their flags, as does Nebraska.

Throw in that ubiquitous blacksmith and Nebraska's state flag is just as appropriate today as when it was designed. Some spoilsports have suggested the adoption of a meaningful, distinctive, and attractive Nebraska state flag. One design that was pictured in the *Omaha World-Herald* depicts **Chimney Rock**, a **National Historic Site** administered by the Nebraska Historical Society. It was a significant landmark on the Oregon Trail, as was Scotts Bluff, some twenty miles to the west.

Scotts Bluff National Monument commemorates a landmark on the Oregon/California Trails and offers some very rugged and scenic terrain. Occasionally we will be asked such questions as, "Did the emigrants ever use buffalo to pull their covered wagons?" or, "Do your rattlesnakes bite?" (as though we had them trained).

Most of our visitation is during the summer months, but our occasional winter visitors are still concerned about snake activity. Sometimes, after sizing up the particular visitor's gullibility, Rangers have launched into an impromptu warning about the dreaded snow snake — the albino rattlesnake which uses its natural camouflage to hide in snow banks. When the Rangers have a listener hooked, they then caution the visitor to watch for the flickering pink tongue, which is the only way this reptile can be seen in the snow. Of course this kind of fun is quickly followed with a disavowal and a legitimate explanation of reptile behavior.

Nebraska's alpine monoliths are connected by a vast expanse of grassland to the Rocky Mountains proper in Wyoming. Except for their scenery, wildlife, flags, history, and life-styles, the two states are quite similar.

116 Wyoming: Women, Volcanic Plugs, and Flags

In 1869, Wyoming became the first state to give women the right to vote, a fact residents proudly advertise through the nickname *Equality State* and the motto "Equal Rights." The state seal is graced by the motto and a picture of a woman. In 1906, Devils Tower — a volcanic monolith which towers above the plains of eastern Wyoming and starred in the movie *Close Encounters of the Third Kind* — was declared the nation's first national monument.

But women and volcanic plugs take a back seat to Wyoming's real claim to fame — **Yellowstone National Park**. The world's first national park was established in 1872, just three years after Wyoming's women were given the right to vote. Most anywhere in America, when conversations turn to national parks, the name Yellowstone is likely to register in peoples' minds.

Wyoming's flag — one of the relatively few state flags that have any class — also reflects a number of firsts. In contrast to most state flags, which were designed by men who didn't know anything about flag design, Wyoming's flag was designed by a young girl, Verna Keays, who first saw it in a dream. Living in a town called Buffalo, she envisioned a bison as part of her design.

Before Verna's vision became official, however, the bison did an about face. She had depicted it facing the fly — the side of a flag not attached to the flagpole. But animals on flags traditionally face the staff. This tradition is appropriate on Wyoming's flag, as bison stoically face into the wind when engulfed in blizzards. Actually, they would be even more stoic if they faced the other way, as their hind quarters lack the shaggy hair that make bison even more distinctive.

The bison on Wyoming's flag is "branded" with the state seal. The blue background suggests the Rocky Mountains. This is also appropriate since the last wild herd of bison in the United States survives in the Yellowstone region, which is located in the Rockies.

It is generally believed that legendary mountain man John Colter was the first white man to see Yellowstone. This occurred during his epic, 500-mile journey — in winter and alone — in 1807. (No stranger to epic journeys, Colter had earlier accompanied Lewis and Clark.)

Yellowstone's fabulous features lent themselves to embellishment around campfires. Yet they didn't need to be embellished — for a long time the outside world didn't believe the *truth* about this geothermal theme park. There was simply nothing to compare it to, the East lacking geysers, wilderness, and wildlife.

The first full-scale Yellowstone expedition was organized in 1870. A party of twenty explorers under the command of Civil War general and congressman Henry D. Washburn penetrated the region and confirmed that it was really neat. Today, millions of visitors from fifty states and numerous foreign nations can empathize with the following account written by the explorers:

> I can scarcely realize that in the unbroken solitude of this majestic range of rocks, away from civilization and almost inaccessible to human approach, the Almighty has placed so many of the most wonderful and magnificent objects of His creation, and that I am to be one of the few first to bring them to the notice of the world.

As the explorers rode along the Firehole River, near the end of their journey, they emerged from a dense forest to encounter a column of steam and water shooting over 100 feet into the sky in an open basin bathed in rising clouds of vapor. They had come face-to-face with that perennial Yellowstone symbol, Old Faithful.

After the expedition's fantastic claims were verified by a second expedition, Yellowstone was declared a national park on March 1, 1972. (President Ulysses S. Grant signed the legislation.) To this day, Yellowstone National Park's birthday is celebrated annually by the eruption of geysers. Old Faithful is just one of some 10,000 geysers and hot springs that make this Earth's greatest geyser area.

Perhaps Wyoming will one day be truly liberated and Yellowstone will have both geysers and galsers. In the meantime, Yellowstone is presumably Earth's greatest spawner of geyser humor.* The following item was contributed by a Park Ranger.

*Do you know any good geyser jokes or stories from either Yellowstone or Iceland? If so, send them to Geyser Tales, Geobopological Survey, PO Box 95465, Seattle, WA 98145

This visitor question is very common at Old Faithful Geyser and many park rangers have experienced it. In 1968, a man in his early thirties, followed by his wife and three pre-teen youngsters, hurriedly approached me at the visitor center and asked, "What time will you be turning the geyser on?" Although sometimes I would like to string the visitor along for my own amusement and say something like, "If the pipes don't break we'll start the show in 20 minutes," I answer honestly and with a straight face, "20 minutes."

An anonymous correspondent contributed the following questions.

Where is the guy that turns the valve that makes Old Faithful erupt?

What comes out of Old Faithful when it erupts?

When's the next erection of Old Faithful?

When do you feed the animals?

How long did it take to build the fence around Yellowstone that keeps all the animals out?

Why do all of the animals stay in the park? Is the entire area of Yellowstone fenced in?

Where did you keep all the animals during the 1988 fires?

Where do you keep the bears at night?

When do the deer turn into elk?

One lady filed a letter of complaint [with whom, the Better Business Bureau?], claiming that Yellowstone is false advertising because she did not see elk in Elk Park, where there's a sign that says "Elk Park."

A lady called and asked if she could roller blade in Yellowstone during the off-season as there is no automobile traffic. She then asked if she were skating along and ran into a herd of buffalo what she should do. I responded, "you know you can't rollerskate in a buffalo herd."

Is there anything to see here?

Can we see all of Yellowstone in just a couple hours?

I see all these entrances, where is the exit?

Can we go nude in Yellowstone?

Why do they call it Fishing Bridge when you can't fish there? Shouldn't it be called "No-Fishing Bridge?"

Where are the presidents' faces?

The following letter, dated July 15, 1987, was addressed to Yellowstone National Park:

This, I know, sounds ridiculous but I'm trying anyway.

I'm 67 years old at present. When I was about 10 years old (1930) our family visited Yellowstone Park.

I left our Black Kodak Box Camera approximately 4 ½" high, 3" wide and 5 ½" long, on a bench, on the front porch of the Main Log Building, I think the main office building near the Yellowstone Falls. We were just starting to move in the transportation vehicle going to see the Yellowstone Falls and I realized and saw the camera sitting there as we drove off. At the time we didn't try to go back.

I guess I've waited a little long to look into the possibility of having that camera in the lost & found department and having it returned to me. At the time, our address was 1023 Lowerline St., New Orleans, La, name _____ [name deleted] my mother. Would you all look around and see if you have or know of the whereabouts of said lost black Kodak Box Camera?

Thank you for indulging me,

[Name deleted]

P.S. Do you all have an up to date map and some historical, with pictures, literature of the park?

Thank you again,

Larry

****

The Tetons rise more than a mile above the sagebrush flats of western Wyoming, creating one of the nation's most famous vistas. It leaves one breathless to imagine what the view must have been like millions of years ago, before erosion whittled the Tetons down to size and built up the surrounding flatlands with their sediments.

"When do the elk turn into moose?" That is one of the questions that left me breathless during my season as a ranger in **Grand Teton National Park**. Of course, mammals don't undergo metamorphosis; that's for amphibians, fishes, and invertebrates. Yet, in a sense, elk did turn into moose in North America.

120   "When do the Elk Turn Into Moose?"

Understand, first of all, that moose and elk both inhabit the Old World as well as the New World. Moose are widespread in Eurasia's boreal forest, while the elk masquerades in the British Isles as the red deer, with related species scattered eastward into India and China. The Norwegian name for the moose is *elk*.

European-American colonists renamed the Norwegian *elk moose* — appropriately from an Algonquian (Indian) name. A beautiful Native American name was popularly used for North America's second largest member of the deer family —*wapiti*, in the Algonquian tongue. The third largest North American deer was named *caribou*, a French-Canadian name which was originally — take a guess — Algonquian.* It was a beautiful scheme. Unfortunately, someone messed it up by calling the *wapiti* by the Norwegian name for moose — *elk*.

If you're confused, just remember that the Norwegian elkhound is bred to hunt the animal North Americans call a moose, while Wyoming's National Elk Refuge — located not far from a community in Grand Teton National Park named Moose (which is too small to boast an Elk's Club) — protects wapiti. An elk and moose are depicted on Michigan's state flag, which is in turn depicted on page 40. Readers looking for a handy field guide to assist them in distinguishing elk from moose are advised to purchase a miniature Michigan state flag. It would be much lighter than this book and, when rolled up, would take up less room than a cellular phone.

Norway's national animal, by the way, is the *elk* — moose to a North American. Oh, and the prehistoric Irish elk you may have heard of was not restricted to Ireland and was neither a moose/*elk* nor an elk/*wapiti*. It was more closely related to the Old World fallow deer.

Even Theodore Roosevelt got into the action. He belonged to the Bull Moose Party, yet lent his name to the Roosevelt elk, a title that later hurt that animal's political career (see page 187).

---

*No, *reindeer* is not Algonquian. It's a Scandinavian term for caribou which North Americans apply to the semidomesticated deer Laplanders herd. The term is hardly relevant in North America where reindeer are virtually unknown, the tradition of herding semidomesticated caribou never having attracted a really strong following here.

It's really important that Americans get their moose and elk straight, for besides being popular targets for photographers and hunters, they rank among our most important symbols and have for some time. One of North America's oldest European cervid emblems is Newfoundland's coat of arms, which is said to depict an "elk" and is therefore misleading, for elk aren't native to Newfoundland.* Perhaps the designer meant to say "moose" or "caribou." Or perhaps he simply didn't care. Newfoundland's arms also depicts two Beothuck Indians — a fine tribute to a race that no longer exists.

A moose is depicted on Maine's state flag and seal, a state of affairs that led to its designation as the *Pine Tree State*'s official animal. Although Michigan's flag unites the moose and elk, it doesn't benefit from their synergy, as the animals appear to have been drawn by a child.**

The elk can survive the humiliation of being caricatured on the flag of a state that is virtually elkless. The elk, as it were — and still is — is depicted on more state flags, seals, and arms than any other native animal except perhaps the horse. (After evolving in North America, the horse died out in America — but not before migrating across the Bering Land Bridge into Eurasia. There, people captured and domesticated horses and returned them to the New World.)

Although many people regard the bison/buffalo as the United States national animal, the elk/wapiti clearly surpasses that animal in popularity as a state emblem. However, no individual elk-depicting emblem matches Wyoming's buffalo flag for grandeur; one almost needs a magnifying glass to see the elk on Oregon's flag.

The elk's symbolic status is not limited to flags and seals. Elk originally ranged from Atlantic to Pacific Coasts, the bison from the Atlantic Coast to the Rocky Mountains. In frontier America, elk were

(Continued on page 124)

*Cervid is a collective term for animals that belong to the deer family, Cervidae.

**It's fine for children to design flags, as they did in Wyoming and Alaska, but I really think professional artists — who are generally adults — ought to be entrusted with putting their visions on cloth. On the other hand, most state flags look like they were designed and sewn by children anyway!

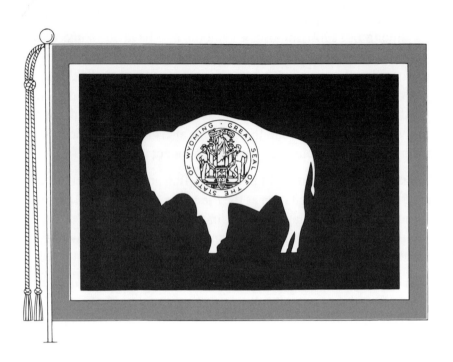

(Above) Wyoming's flag is a classic. The blue background suggests the Rocky Mountains, which are actually in Wyoming. The bison suggests two things: 1) bison, and 2) roller-skating — in a buffalo herd.

(Opposite page, top) Chimney Rock graces the author's suggested Nebraska state flag, a modification of a design created by Nebraskan school teacher Don Frederick and featured in the Omaha *World-Herald* (October 25, 1992). The background colors could be yellow sandwiched by green — suggestive of an ear of corn, agriculture, and the nickname *Cornhuskers*. Or Scotts Bluff could be set against a white stripe representing snow snakes. Outer blue stripes could represent the distant Rocky Mountains and the Coast Ranges beyond. And there's plenty of room for the blacksmith from Nebraska's present flag.

(Opposite page, bottom) Scotts Bluff is an alpine wonderland which provides important habitat for the critically endangered Nebraska snow snake. Environmentalists have blocked plans to turn Scotts Bluff into Nebraska's first ski resort.

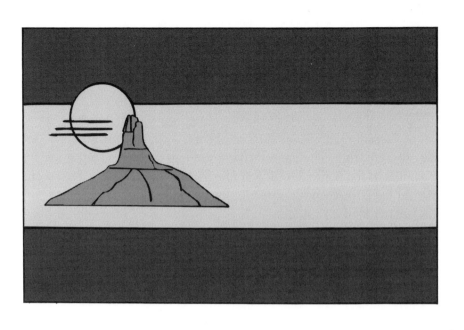

apparently more popular than bison, at least east of the Missouri River, for there are many more communities named for elk than for bison — which are almost unanimously named "Buffalo." Buffalo, New York, is an exception — as well as outside the bison's original range. Perhaps Elk is simply more euphonious than Buffalo — or did people favor Elk because it's so compact?

In Wyoming, however, buffalo and elk — each a misnomer — are on equal footing. The nation's most famous herd of wapiti graze the pastures of the National Elk Refuge, in the shadow of the Tetons and not far from the community of Jackson, which boasts a park featuring arches made of elk antlers.

Inspired by their state flag, Wyoming school children successfully promoted the "American bison-bison buffalo" — that's exactly how they worded it — for adoption as Wyoming's official state mammal.*

****

During my tour of duty at Grand Teton National Park, I was walking through a campground when a woman called me over and asked me to identify an unusually large fungus growing on her campsite. I commented, "I have no idea what that is. Sure is a big one, huh?" "Yea," she replied, as she put her foot on it and squashed it.

A windstorm had toppled acres of timber a few years earlier. We were tormented for two or three days by a guest who just couldn't understand why he shouldn't be allowed to take his chain saw and do something useful with all that wood. He didn't seem to think the other campers would mind the noise. Puh-leezzzz!!

****

Who says the United States government didn't care about conservation in the 19th century? The federal government conferred national park status on Yellowstone four years before it allowed Colorado to become a state. Residents were hurt when they realized their government cared more about bison and geysers than people. But Colorado's resilient citizens — hardened by blizzards and avalanches — had the last laugh.

*Can you imagine if Buffalo Bill had been named American Bison-Bison Buffalo William?

"Colorado is known as the *Centennial State* because it attained statehood in 1876, the one-hundredth-year anniversary of the signing of the Declaration of Independence," according to one reference and doubtless confirmed by others. But Colorado is much better known for its mountains than for historical coincidences.

Colorado is world-renowned for its beautiful aspen trees and ski slopes. These two heavyweight symbols are united in Aspen, Colorado, which attracts a large percentage of the world's *beautiful people* every winter. For people who can't afford to hop on a Learjet and fly to Aspen for the weekend, Colorado boasts another dual symbol that is accessible to us commoners — Denver.

This name represents both a mile-high city and a mile-high singer. Denver, the *Mile-High City*, is Colorado's capital. The singer is John Denver, of course. How can you hear the name John Denver and not think about snow-capped peaks, soaring eagles, power lines snapped by blizzards, frozen toes, and ecologically-sound wildlife management practices?

Rocky Mountain National Park could have no more appropriate home than Colorado. If I told you that Rocky Mountain National Park was established in honor of John Denver, you'd probably believe me, but it wasn't. The park was established in 1915, before John was even born. In keeping with John Denver's hit song *Rocky Mountain High*, Rocky Mountain National Park is the source of some very lofty humor. The following items were submitted by Douglas Caldwell, Rocky Mountain National Park's Public Information Officer.

Nearly one-third of Rocky Mountain National Park's 265,727 acres is above treeline (11,000 feet). This area — the tundra, Russian for "land of no trees' — is covered by low growing plants, an adaptation to the extremes of wind and cold. To someone new to the tundra, it gives a well kept look. Undoubtedly, this leads to the question, which our rangers hear nearly every summer, "How many times a summer does the park mow the tundra?"

Instead of getting the question, "When do the deer turn into moose," we are asked, "When do the deer turn into elk?" Near the end of a busy summer's day, a seasonal ranger could no longer resist the temptation, and responded, "On October 15." So, somewhere out there in America is someone who swears that according to a ranger in Rocky Mountain National Park, the deer change into elk on October 15 of each year.

Two summers ago, one of our rangers at the information desk in the Park Headquarters Visitor Center was asked what is the best time of the day for viewing elk? The ranger responded, "Just after sunrise, or about an hour before sunset are good times to watch the elk, because at mid-day, they rest in the trees (i.e., the elk seek refuge from the heat of the day under the canopy of the park's trees)." "Oh," the visitor responded, "I didn't know elk can climb trees!" So, we have to be careful about how we express ourselves to our visitors!

****

Fossils of plants and animals are found in the Rocky Mountains. **Florissant Fossil Beds National Monument**, Colorado preserves a wealth of remarkably well preserved fossil insects, seeds, and leaves, along with an unusual display of standing petrified sequoia stumps. These may sound lackluster compared to the West's great dinosaur boneyards. But Florissant's fossils are distinguished by their remarkable degree of preservation. The fossils date back more than twenty million years to the Oligocene Epoch, an era also represented by the mammals whose bones decorate South Dakota's Badlands. A Park Ranger reminds us that prehistoric parks can be philosophical.

A visitor asked, "Are we here?" referring to the fact that the fossil beds are not obvious. But the ranger, in a humorous note, responded: "If you're not, I sure have a good imagination!"

These bighorn sheep are clashing heads after having run at each other as fast as they can. Such eminently irrational behavior makes one wonder if mammals really represent an evolutionary advance over coldblooded animals. Wildlife photographer Jeff Foott took this picture in America's largest wilderness preserve, Canada.

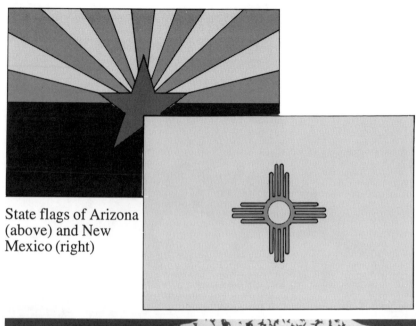

State flags of Arizona (above) and New Mexico (right)

Many visitors to New Mexico's Carlsbad Caverns National Park say the daily bat flights remind them of Pearl Harbor. Check out the photo on page 168. All things are truly connected.

THE SOUTHWEST
Land of Enchanted Tourists

My first encounter with the Southwest was heavenly. Vast patches of desert streaked by below me, punctuated by irrational landforms that seemed to reach up to grab me. Even at 10,000 feet above sea level, the air reeked of pinyons, cacti, roadrunners, rattlesnakes. Exhilarated by the fantasy of light, rock, speed, and Earth scents, I zoomed in for a closer look at my native planet, even as I maneuvered my craft into a series of every wilder gyrations.

Glimpsing a jet off the port bow, I was reminded that I was passing dangerously close to a missile testing range. A smoke ring hanging listlessly in the sky told me that my distant companion had changed course... There he was streaking towards me! A second jet joined the chase to starboard. I put my Cessna into a power dive and gunned the engine, at the same time going into a roll. I ignored the alarms and flashing lights that warned of danger as the boundary between Earth and Sky blurred.

Suddenly, I heard screaming and furious pounding on the window. Pain wracked my body as I struggled to sit up, squinting desperately through a swollen eye. Thank God rescuers were on hand to rescue me from my flaming craft!

I was shocked back to reality by a familiar — and not too friendly — face beckoning me. I stepped out of the flight simulator.

"If this were a *real* plane, you would have died before takeoff!" the flight instructor growled at me. "If this piece of junk was a *real* plane, I wouldn't have been flying upside down fifty feet below sea level, moron," I snapped back at the arrogant flight instructor.

As I stepped outside into another rainy Seattle day, I reflected on the preceding events. A lot of so-called experts remind me of that flight instructor. They have a lot of knowledge and maybe even a steady paycheck, but they just don't get the big picture. Are you a flight instructor or a thinker and a doer? If you live in a world of simulated flight and virtual reality, then you probably think this book is little more than a humorous look at wilderness, tourism, and America.

If, on the other hand, your feet are on the ground and you've read this far, you've probably discovered that this book isn't about wilderness, tourists, or humor at all. It's really about flags.

I wrote earlier of a connection between flags and wilderness; most state flags east of the Missouri River are as mundane as the civilized landscapes they represent, while several sensational flags flourish in the West. State flags reach their zenith in the sunny Southwest. Texas' *Lone Star* banner rules a region lying partly within the Southwest. Oklahoma is sometimes classified as a Southwest state as well.

Flags get even better in the heart of the Southwest. Perhaps the most elegant of state flags — certainly one of the most distinctive — represents the *Land of Enchantment*. New Mexico's flag depicts an ancient Zia Indian sun emblem against a yellow background. One can hardly look at New Mexico's flag without thinking of sunshine, glowing rocks, and ancient legends. It is truly a *Flag of Enchantment*.

But beauty is in the eye of the beholder. One of the nation's foremost vexillographers (flag designer) lives less than a mile away from me here in Seattle. Gary Csillaghegyi was an astronomer before he began designing flags. Not the type to simply stare through telescopes, he had ambitions of going to Mars before his position with NASA was axed due to budget cuts. (Many of our state flags belong on Mars.)

Like me, Gary appreciates flags adorned with heavenly bodies. However, his favorite state flag belongs not to New Mexico, but to Arizona. (One of Gary's favorite national flags is Brazil's, with its star-studded globe.) Arizona's flag features a copper-colored star — symbolic of Arizona's great wealth in copper — against red and yellow diagonal stripes suggesting a rising or setting sun above, a solid blue background below.*

Gary made and sold an Imperial Russian flag to a Romanov for $11,000. The Romanovs, as you may know, were the last Russian royal family. Few people other than royalty can afford an $11,000 flag. Despite his talent and status, Gary's business is hardly thriving,

Actually, most of Gary's flags cost far less than $11,000, but they still typically cost more than most people care to spend on flags. The cheap flags that most people fly in their backyards or in parades are just that — cheap. Flags that can be valued as conversation pieces or heirlooms may cost a few hundred or thousand dollars, depending on the materials and detail of the design.

---

*Gary corrects me: "The array of 13 red and yellow beams behind the copper star is called a gyrony. Diagonal isn't really correct. Actually it is supposed to be a red sky with gold beams streaming through it."

At any rate, I thought I would include Gary's address for readers who may be looking for someone capable of making a flag the way flags are meant to be made. I owe it to him, because he related to me one of the few humorous tourist questions I received that relate to the Southwest. And after he reviewed my manuscript with that single question from Petrified Forest National Park, Gary unleashed a barrage of material on me.

If you're the type who likes to buck the crowd — an individualist — and are lucky enough to live in an uncivilized state like Nebraska, Idaho, or Washington, have Gary make one of the proposed flags that are featured in this book. Who knows, you may be flying a future state flag in your back yard. It will certainly be far superior to the current state flag and may be a collector's item someday.

I had set this space aside for Gary Csillaghegyi's address. Just before this book went to press, I learned that he had passed away. Although a book based on humor hardly seems a fitting medium for paying last respects, this book does include a deeper message which I think befits a thinker and vexillographer of Gary's stature.

Gary had a keen interest in symbolism. Csillaghegyi (CHIL.log. hedge.yee) means "star mountain" in Hungarian, thus Gary's company name — *Starflag*. In *Desert Solitaire*, Edward Abbey recalled a song made up by captive Zia Indians which symbolically unites mountains, stars (through its connection to the Zia sun emblem on New Mexico's flag), and loss:

> My home over there,
> Now I remember it;
> And when I see that mountain far away,
> Why then I weep,
> Why then I weep,
> Remembering my home.

As remembrance, reflection, and weeping symbolize grief, so are release and laughter representative of grief's counterpart, which can also be noble. As Abbey noted, "Where there is no joy there can be no courage; and without courage all other virtues are useless." After reviewing my manuscript, Gary said "I laughed myself hoarse."

Besides flags, this book is also about the irrational questions the public asks when visiting America's wilderness preserves. Some of the nation's most irrational national parks and monuments, including the best known preserves in the Southwest, have been carved out of a vast landform geologists call the Colorado Plateau. (I use the same term.) This region covers an immense area of Colorado, Utah, New Mexico, and Arizona.

Anyone who knows that a plateau is an elevated flattish area may think "Colorado Plateau" is an irrational name when gazing at the tortured terrain showcased in the Grand Canyon, Bryce Canyon, or Zion. Millions of years ago, the region *was* flattish and therefore presumably boring. (Is that why dinosaurs became extinct?)

Fortunately, powerful forces elevated the region, converting it to a plateau. Gravity must work harder to drag upland rivers down to the sea than to pull their lowland kin into the drink. The Colorado Plateau's rivers tore at the limestones and sandstones that are so common here, like worms burrowing through cheese. The arid climate helped shape those distinctive Southwest landforms. (One can only wonder what the Southwest might look like if it was subjected to the Pacific Northwest's rainfall. Can you imagine moss-draped arches acting as bridges over rivers overflown by hummingbirds, parrots, and giant butterflies and a Grand Canyon studded with giant shelf fungi?)

The single greatest agent of erosion in the Southwest is the Colorado River, which carved the Grand Canyon. Incidentally, *Colorado* is Spanish for "red." The colors red and yellow in the flags of New Mexico and Arizona suggest early Spanish explorers.

Some of the earliest Spanish explorers in the Southwest were driven by a fabulous quest. Having failed to find the East Indies, then having failed to find a fountain of youth in Florida, they sought compensation in the Southwest in the form of Native American cities made of silver and gold. Does this give you some insight into the Conquistadors' genius? Can you imagine how hot a house made of metal would get in summer in the Southwest? Native Americans might have rid themselves of their unwelcome hosts if they had only started rumors of cities of gold at the bottom of the sea.

Perhaps I should lighten up. After all, if I encountered peasant farmers wandering barefoot in a barren environment, I would probably assume they lived in cities made of silver and gold, also. Moreover, Spanish explorers did succeed in discovering the elusive Grand Canyon. This is fortunate, for without its discovery the National Park Service's empire would be missing one of its most popular attractions, **Grand Canyon National Park**, and Arizona would have no nickname. And this book would not feature a chapter on Grand Canyon humor.

Come to think of it, it *doesn't* feature such a chapter. Sadly, I received just four questions inspired by this epic fissure. The first two were allegedly fielded by a wrangler prior to a mule ride down into the Grand Canyon on the Bright Angel Trail.

Do you have a dining car on the mule train?

Where are the elevators to the bottom of the canyon?

Is there RV parking at Phantom Ranch?

What time do they turn the lights on in the canyon?

Can any readers send me two or three more one-liners from the Grand Canyon for my sequel?

****

As I entered the *peetrified* forest of Arizona, I saw *peetrified* birds a settin' on *peetrified* trees, a singin' *peetrified* songs in the *peetrified* air. The flowers, leaves and grass also was *peetrified*. And they shone in a *peeculiar* moonglow — which wuz *peetrified*, too.
— Jim Bridger, renowned trapper and mountain man, circa 1850 (probably apocryphal and written in reference to Yellowstone, which also has petrified wood and which Jim Bridger actually visited)

If a joke is told in a wilderness that is so remote there is no one to hear it, is it funny? If a joke was told millions of years before humans evolved, would it have been funny? If a joke is told millions of years in the future, after humanity has been exterminated by nuclear warfare, biological warfare, or simply a mass loss of the will to live, will it be funny?

These are philosophical questions for which science has no answer. But they can be pondered in Arizona's **Petrified Forest National Park**, for it is remote, old, and durable. How remote? It's in Arizona; even mountain man Jim Bridger never visited it. How old? The trees for which the park is named grew some 225 million years ago, when dinosaurs were just beginning their reign of terror. How durable? Bite a piece of petrified wood, the ultimate hardwood.

No one at Petrified Forest National Park sent me any material for this book. But on May 1, 1995 I had the good fortune to learn of a humorous visitor's question while standing in a post office in Seattle.

A man approached and greeted me, and I looked up to see Gary Csillaghegyi. Gary is an astronomer, vexillologist, and, apparently, a paleontologist. Moreover, he is or has been an active participant in these endeavors, rather than an armchair observer — Gary ranks as one of the nation's top vexillographers, once dreamed of being a tourist on Mars, and excavated a phytosaur. (Incidentally, I have also dreamed of going to Mars, though I've had little opportunity, not having had a position with NASA.) Phytosaurs were crocodile-like animals that lived during the Triassic Period, when Petrified Forest National Park's trees were growing and photosynthesizing and dinosaurs were as novel as sensible state flags.

I told Gary that I was writing a book about flags, supplemented with a few humorous tourist questions. Gary said his father had once worked as a ranger at Petrified Forest National Park. He remembered his father laughing about the visitors who asked, "Where are the trees?"* The trees are there. They're just disoriented, as are many visitors, politicians, environmentalists, and anti-environmentalists.

---

*Who would have thought, millions of years ago, that primitive trees would evolve into species from whose wood paper can be made and that a highly-advanced organism would write a book made of such paper that features a silly question people ask about those primitive trees? And who would have thought the author would have heard that question from an astronomer/vexillographer who excavated a phytosaur in a post office in Seattle, which is in a state where there is nothing *but* trees? The circle will be complete if someone reads only this paragraph, believes that a phytosaur was excavated in a post office, and convinces the *National Enquirer* to write about it! And what if people begin tearing up post offices across the country and someone *does* find a phytosaur? Do we live in a wondrous universe or what?

The trees commemorated in Petrified Forest National Park rivaled California's redwoods in stature. Can you imagine how much mud or volcanic ash it would take to bury a redwood forest? There are places where tree *stumps* are preserved upright, some even harboring fossilized animal residents (Nova Scotia comes to mind). But the wood in Petrified Forest National Park, like most petrified wood, is horizontal.

The visitors who asked where Petrified Forest National Park's trees are can hardly be blamed, for the Park's name is misleading. It might be called Ironic National Forest, but that would only cause visitors to ask where the trees made of iron are. It should be called Petrified *Wood* National Park. On second thought, *Fossilized* Wood National Park sounds more professional. But "Park" might deceive visitors into thinking they can eat a picnic lunch under shade trees while looking at fossilized wood. If the National Park Service is as serious about environmental education as it professes to be, it will redesignate this unit Fossilized Wood National Treeless Area. Finally, this name could be shortened to Fossilized Wood National Tundra, since *tundra* means treeless area.

This is not a trivial issue. Certain National Park Service personnel criticized me for writing a book that "makes fun of tourists," then they go and dupe visitors with a name like Petrified Forest National Park. And get this — there is now a Petrified Forest National Park in Argentina! Are people going to begin designating Petrified Forest national parks wherever they find a piece of petrified wood? There is already a Ginkgo Petrified Forest State Park in Washington (State). Desperate for tourist attractions, Dakotans might latch onto this publicity gimmick and jointly designate the two states Dakota Petrified Forest National Park.* (Actually, this might not be a bad idea. Shaking down tourists entering South Dakota for admission fees might take a chunk out of our national debt.)

In this age of unrelenting litigation, when lawyers are nearly as abundant as the great bison herds that once roamed the Great Plains, the National Park Service could — and perhaps should — be sued for designating such an inappropriate name. Under threat of such a law-

---

*North Dakota's official state fossil is teredo petrified wood, essentially wood that was bored by prehistoric "shipworms." A teredo petrified wood pendant would make a fine gift for a graduate of a Belle Fourche Navel Academy.

suit, however, the National Park Service might simply relinquish its claim to Petrified/Fossilized Forest/Wood National Park/Tundra and the public would lose one of the most economical units in the organization's empire. The beautiful thing about petrified forests is that they don't burn; this is not Smokey Bear country. (The original Smokey Bear hailed from neighboring New Mexico, by the way.) Taxpayers don't have to finance firefighters in Petrified Forest National Park! Indeed, there are rumors that jealous USDA Forest Service administrators are searching for their own fossilized timber farm. Will they call it Petrified Park National Forest?

Incidentally, most of the fossilized wood found in Petrified Forest National Park derives from an extinct conifer, *Araucarioxylon arizonicum*. More commonly known as Arizona petrified wood, its fossilized wood is Arizona's official state fossil.

Among the most beautiful of trees, living araucarians are native to the Southern Hemisphere. They include South America's monkey puzzle tree — which thrives here in Seattle — the bunya-bunya tree (the name rhymes with *gunya-gunya free*), New Zealand's Kawri pine, and the Norfolk Island pine. Of the last, it has been said, "They are to trees what Mount Fuji is to volcanoes." This doesn't mean that Norfolk Island pines are commonly climbed by Japanese tourists, for Norfolk Island is off the coast of Australia; the comparison is to Mt. Fuji's beauty and symmetry. A Norfolk Island pine is the central motif on Norfolk Island's flag.

But this book isn't about flags that depict aberrantly beautiful trees from islands few people have heard of. It's about *America*, and this chapter is about America's *Fabulous Flag Belt*, the Southwest. And it is particularly about Arizona's Petrified Forest National Park, where there are few trees to depict on flags. Gary Csillaghegyi offers more prehistoric non-arboreal humor.

> Could we get some cuttings in the trading post and start our own tree at home?
>
> Do the petrified logs burn slowly, like oak? And do they make pretty colors, like when you put salt and things in a fire? (Arizona petrified wood is renowned for its beautiful colors.)

(I've thrown a great variety of things in people's fireplaces, but never salt. I'll have to try it sometime. I need to get a fireplace first — or get invited back to a friend's home.)

Gary comments on the "so-called 'picture wood' that arises where the core of the tree has partly decayed before fossilization and has beautiful moss or frost-pattern like patterns fossilized in different minerals. The beauty can be especially brought out by judicious slicing of the log, and mirror-finish polishing. Even in the rough state, though, the stuff is striking. The museum has many examples of finished stuff; but you can find big pieces almost anywhere, especially in the Rainbow Forest."* This dazzling picture wood inspired another question:

Do you do the inlay work here?

Gary continues.

A lot of early prospectors dynamited hundreds of logs in search of diamonds at their cores. For this reason there are millions of chips scattered all around the areas where there are lots of logs exposed, especially in the Rainbow Forest just behind the museum, and similar places. Many a tourist asked on seeing this mess, and the truly titanic logs laying around those areas: "Did the Indians cut them down?"

As a public service, I wish to advise readers that it is now illegal to dynamite petrified wood in Petrified Forest National Park in search of diamonds, platinum, gold, silver, or mother-of-pearl. There are, however, locations outside the Park where petrified wood can be found or bought. You can take it home and dynamite it, if you want. If you live in an uptight community that has a city ordinance restricting the use of dynamite, you could probably sneak onto one of the countless weapons testing ranges that litter the Southwest and do it.

Public Service Announcement #2: Trespassing on these reservations is illegal. But why let the government spend your tax dollars on missiles and bombs to defend your freedom if you can't exercise that freedom by dynamiting petrified wood in the Desert Southwest?

If trees hadn't been so damned common back in the Triassic, Petrified Forest National Park might be known as Petrified *Phytosaur* National Park. Gary recalls a couple questions that referred to the "fossil phytosaurs and other Triassic animals in the museum (including a beautiful diorama)."

Do you still have any of these around? Should we watch out for them?

*Author's question: Is Rainbow Forest only visible after rainstorms?

Most books about humorous tourist questions in America's wilderness wonderlands would simply let it go at that. Yet even though this book's primary topic is flags, I will nevertheless take the time to offer professional answers that can and ought to be used to deal with such questions in the future. In answer to the first question, I would respond, "Yes, (Sir, Mam, etc.) — they're still around, but they're no longer living; they've become fossils." In answer to the second question, I would ask, "If you don't watch out for them, who will?"

And "from the Painted Desert, up at the north end of the Park, where tourists come to the Painted Desert Inn and get their first sight of the Bentonite hills across the rim."* —

"Does the Park Service repaint them every so often? Do they do it by plane, like crop dusting?" God's truth!, Dave, someone asked that of the innkeeper at one point. . . . I remember sitting in the Inn coffee shop while he [Andy Gould, the innkeeper] ran me up a nice, cold chocolate malt, and telling me about it just happening a few hours previously. We laughed about that one for days. . . . This was in 1949 or 50, I think.**

In fact, the question about the crop-dusting plane is not so silly. For if the National Park Service did decide to paint the Southwest — why not, Borglum sculpted Mt. Rushmore and people bored holes through California redwoods; let's put Devils Tower on a potter's wheel and glaze it! — they certainly would not and could not do it by hand. Aerial spraying is the only feasible means of painting a desert.

Gary contributes a not-so-humorous anecdote.

When I was growing up, one of the more valued pieces in the Museum was a sphere of black onyx about 15 cm. in diameter. It had been cut from a piece with two parallel narrow bands of white in it, in such a manner that the white lines formed the North and South polar circles of an imaginary world globe. I don't think the outlines of the continents were etched on it, just the natural white bands to form the circles. This little gem had been the gift to the Petrified Forest of Kaiser Wilhelm II about 1912 or so. During the early years of the

*No, these hills do not resemble suitcases. You're thinking of *Samsonite.*

**Attention future contributors of humorous tourist questions: Please be precise with your dates. In the sequel, I will be less tolerant of this "I think" crap.

Kennedy admin., when Stuart Udall (an Arizonan of one of our grand old families — his aunt was my fourth grade teacher, and his uncle was Superior Court Judge in Holbrook, near where we lived then) was Secretary of the Interior, the Petrified Forest was upgraded from Monument to Park, and a new museum was built. In 1964, after graduation from College, before going out to UCLA, I dragged my college roommate out to see the place and show off my early home. Of course, I took him into the museum to show him its treasures, including the Kaiser's Sphere. It wasn't there. I checked with the curator to see whether or not it had been put in storage, or loaned to another museum, or sent to the Smithsonian...(?). They had no record in the inventory of the museum. I raised a yelp, and nearly got us thrown out of the Park. When we got home I wrote a letter to Senator Goldwater explaining the whole thing. He said he would look into it, but I never pursued it or found out what happened, or where or if the thing turned up. But...that was one of our little National Treasures — at least in my opinion.

On another serious note, I'm curious as to how the folks at Petrified Forest National Park celebrate Arbor Day. Do they just get stoned?

P.S. A Park Ranger from Petrified Forest National Park, responds to my charge that the Park is misnamed.

> Over the years, various alternate names have been suggested for Petrified Forest National Park. However, none provide a better picture of the features or improve the designation. In 1906 when Congress established Petrified Forest National Monument (predecessor to the present national park), it was established to protect the remains of the Mesozoic forests. They were thinking of the fossilized wood, but ironically hit the nail on the head by protecting all the remains of the forests. Over the years, scientists have studied the Triassic Chinle formation and as a result, we have an ever-growing picture of the environment of 225 million years ago: forests with fossilized plants, reptiles, fish, clams, and early dinosaurs. So the designation as a Petrified Forest and as a national park is appropriate despite the seemingly erroneous name. Once visitors understand the complete story, they support Petrified Forest National Park.

140   Carlsbad Caverns: Woodstock Turned Sour

****

Imagine you're snorkeling off Australia's Great Barrier Reef. Your companion gestures at you and appears to be mouthing words, but you can't understand him underwater. So you surface.

Frantically removing his mask, your companion blabbers, "Imagine, *moit* (mate), if the Great Barrier Reef was lifted above sea level, buried under sediments, fossilized, and *loiter* eroded internally by underground rivulets. Imagine that millions of winged mammals colonized the fossilized reef and that people *coim* to mine their droppings for use in warfare. And *loiter* still, people poisoned the winged mammals, though tourists still *coim* to witness the spectacle afforded by the survivors."

Of course, you'd think your companion is insane. But his prediction has already come true in the *Land of Enchantment*, New Mexico. There — or here, if you're reading this in New Mexico — water has eroded one of Earth's great caverns out of what was once a reef.* It is known as **Carlsbad Caverns** and has been designated a **National Park**. The winged mammals? Scientists call them bats, and there are thousands of them.

If the spectacle of thousands of bats pouring out of a cave at dusk doesn't stimulate your imagination, then translate it into human terms: This scenario is eerily reminiscent of Woodstock.

Try to imagine one million people spending the day in a cave, hanging upside down (naked), then emerging en masse at dusk (still naked). On top of that, imagine all one million people running, twisting, and dodging while screaming at the top of their lungs, hoping to hear their voices echo off tiny, flying insects. Try it sometime. It's not as easy as it sounds.

Readers who believe that humans dominate Earth might think that Carlsbad Caverns was surpassed by Woodstock, where an estimated

---

*To impress upon visitors the fact that Carlsbad Caverns was once a reef I've suggested to Park Service personnel that they offer visitors glass-bottom boat tours in some of the larger chambers. The federal bureaucracy being what it is, they never responded.

460,000 revelers witnessed musicians assaulting the air waves with electrified music. But guess what — in 1936 the underground pageant that is Carlsbad boasted an estimated *8,700,000* bats. Imagine more than eighteen Woodstocks — in a cave! Moreover, an estimated 25 to 50 million bats once inhabited Arizona's Eagle Cave, with 100 million residing in thirteen caves in Texas!

All the rock concerts that have shattered the peace and quiet that once insulated the North American wilderness since Thomas Edison invented or discovered electricity combined pale next to the spectacle of hundreds of millions of bats that have been turning Southwestern night skies into maelstroms of mindless screaming and voracious feeding frenzies since before our forbears began experimenting with Bluegrass music in the Appalachians.*

The Southwest's nocturnal, aerial Woodstocks are more subdued nowadays. What went wrong? Pesticides. The myth of the pristine Southwest rings false in the ears of the myriad bats who have died wretched deaths, poisoned by chemicals devised by humans to destroy the insects bats evolved to prey on. Apparently, Americans decided that more than 100 million bats that worked without pay, created no serious environmental side-effects, and didn't threaten the health of humans just weren't doing a good enough job.

So thanks to pesticides, human beings are truly #1. Unless you want to consider social insects — ants, termites, bees, and wasps — whose colonies also number in the millions. But people who feel threatened by these six-legged upstarts need not worry. Pesticides will take care of them, too.

A spoilsport at Carlsbad Caverns National Park reminds me that some insects have developed a resistance to pesticides which, in addition, are directly impacting the health of humans. Such negativity! Americans' can-do attitude combined with technology offers an obvious solution to half of this dilemma: Invent new pesticides. And what's more important, healthy people or a healthy economy?

*Edison National Historic Site is in West Orange, New Jersey.

How could the United States abandon our friends the bats? There are those who believe the federal government views Carlsbad's bats as traitors. First of all, the species that I've been describing is known as the Mexican free-tailed bat (*Remember the Alamo!*). Moreover its scientific name, *Tadarida brasiliensis*, commemorates Brazil. Other bats inhabit Carlsbad Caverns, but it is the Mexican freetail that rules the roost.

The Mexican freetail's Southern sympathies were confirmed during the Civil War when the Confederate Army mined bat *guano* (feces, scat, manure, waste, doodoo, etc.). In fairness, I must point out that Confederate guano was mined in caves elsewhere in the Southwest. Most of Carlsbad's guano was mined long after the war for application to newly established citrus groves in Southern California. An estimated 200,000 tons of guano were mined from Carlsbad Caverns over a period of 20 years.

The Confederates didn't use bat guano to launch Florida's citrus industry. Rather, they used it as a source of niter (sodium nitrate) for gunpowder. That one of Nature's wondrous creations could be turned to as foul a purpose as war assaults the senses. The efforts of countless millions of bats over God knows how many centuries went up in smoke on the battlefields of the Civil War. The National Park Service ought to hire someone to sculpt a giant marble bat monument, commemorating both natural history and America's unnatural history. If no one in the South wants it, they can put it in South Dakota.

Once ignited in warfare or converted to orange juice, bat guano can only be replaced by bats. Putting two and two together illustrates a shocking reality: Earth's lost bat guano reserves can scarcely be replaced if bats are being lost to pesticides. The next time you serve your family orange juice, ask them to think about bat guano and pesticides and say a little prayer.

But for the whims of history, the Mexican free-tailed bat might today rank alongside ballistic missiles and nuclear submarines as a standard weapon of destruction, rather than a nostalgic symbol of the Civil War. Consider the following letter.

My Dear Mr. President:

I attach hereto a proposal designed to frighten, demoralize, and excite the prejudices of the people of the Japanese Empire.

As fantastic as you may regard the idea, I am convinced it will work and I earnestly request that it receive the utmost careful consideration, lest our busy leaders overlook a practical, inexpensive, and effective plan to the disadvantage of our armed forces and to the sorrow of the mothers of America. It is one that might easily be used against us if the secret is not carefully guarded.

I urge you to appoint a committee to study thoroughly and promptly all the possibilities of this plan and that its members shall consist of civilians eminently qualified to not only pass upon, but solve all technical matters and recommend methods for the execution of the raids.

After nominating scholars and businessmen to head various departments that would be involved, the author attached this description of his devilish scheme:

Proposal for surprise attack
"REMEMBER PEARL HARBOR"

Shall the sun set quickly over "the land of the rising sun"? I would return the call of the Japanese at Pearl Harbor on December 7, 1941, with a dawn visit at a convenient time in an appropriate way...

The...lowest form of animal life is the BAT, associated in history with the underworld and regions of darkness and evil. Until now reasons for its creation have remained unexplained.

As I vision it the millions of bats that have for ages inhabited our belfries, tunnels and caverns were placed there by God to await this hour to play their part in the scheme of free human existence, and to frustrate any attempt of those who dare desecrate our way of life.

This lowly creature, the bat, is capable of carrying in flight a sufficient quantity of incendiary material to ignite a fire.

The letter suggested a fantastic scenario: Imagine millions of bats armed with small firebombs being released an hour before dawn above a Japanese industrial city... Unseen, the tiny commandoes descend on the city, infiltrating homes and factories. Residents leaving their homes for work might see a million flames erupt simultaneously.

The effect of the destruction from such a mysterious source would be a shock to the morale of the Japanese people as no amount of [ordinary] bombing could accomplish...It would render the Japanese people homeless and their industries useless, yet the innocent could escape with their lives...

If the use of bats in this all-out war can rid us of the Japanese pests, we will, as the Mormons did for the gull at Salt Lake City, erect a monument to their everlasting memory.

The letter suggests that hibernating bats could be easily collected, armed, and transported with minimal feeding or care. The torpid mammals could be activated just prior to release by warming.

In submitting this proposal it is with a fervent prayer that the plan will effectively be used to the everlasting benefit of mankind.

Yours humbly,

Lytle S. Adams

Call it hare-brained, crazy like a fox, or just plain batty, Doc Adams' idea evolved into Project-X. One of the participants, Jack Couffer, describes it in his book *Bat Bomb*. It is appropriate that this book is published by the University of Texas Press, for Texas was a major bat-collecting site for members of the Project-X team. Although they collected a few bats at Carlsbad Caverns, they were reluctant to pillage an important tourist attraction. Besides, how could their project remain secret if tourists witnessed team members making off with millions of bats? They could hardly have passed themselves off as *humaniacs* — animal rights activists — as they were aberrations in those days. (Come to think of it, they're still aberrations.)

Does stateside duty at a time when Americans were sacrificing their lives on remote Pacific islands sound like a treat? Guess again. The author describes what it's like to be urinated on by one million bats, followed by a fecal hailstorm. (Southwest caves may be Earth's largest *batrooms.)*

If this sounds like a foul experience, be advised that the team members endured with the knowledge that their scheme had already been proven sound. In an experiment gone awry, armed kamikaze bats had earlier incinerated Carlsbad Auxiliary Airfield.

Was it this treachery that induced the Pentagon to scrap bats in favor of atoms? For Project-X was competing against the American/ Nazi race to harness the atom. And we know who won. (At least, I do.)

As Couffer points out in his book, a bat holocaust might have allowed Japanese to walk away from burning homes and factories. Certainly, there would have been no lingering radiation nightmares.

What about the bats? They would have humanely fried themselves. Engineering their escape would have meant an even crueler fate — permanent exile in Japan. For it is not likely that the United States government would have authorized their recapture and return to Texas.

But where might a bat-borne victory had led? "It is amusing to visualize the great industrialized nations of the world squabbling over bat caves," writes Couffer.

Could you sleep comfortably knowing that ballistic missiles filled with millions of bats were targeted at your home? Could the bats sleep comfortably? Imagine Carlsbad's rangers replaced by marines who shoot tourists on sight. Imagine small cavern chambers deployed on railroad tracks. Remember that there are ruthless leaders — madmen — who would unleash such a holocaust without batting an eye.

And realize that bat-bombing is a form of biological warfare. Geneticists may soon breed explosive microorganisms. Can you imagine a world where people can't plant seeds, brush their teeth, or flush toilets for fear of blowing up the neighborhood? Antiterrorist personnel would be exhausted defusing nuclear amoebas and protozoans.

It is fortunate that Einstein harnessed the atom, thereby delivering humanity from the specter of international bat/microbe terrorism. The tragedy of the Mexican free-tail bats is quickly forgotten with a couple questions from Carlsbad Caverns National Park.

Are all the caves underground? Have all the caves in the park been discovered?

Here's my suggested response: "All the caves that have so far been discovered are underground — but there's a lot of unexplored territory beyond the lithosphere."

New Mexico's **Capulin Volcano National Monument** showcases the symmetrical cinder cone of a geologically recent, inactive volcano. Neal Bullington, Chief of Interpretation, Sleeping Bear Dunes National Lakeshore, offers a treasure trove of Capulin wit.

When I was working as a Park Ranger at Capulin Mountain National Monument in New Mexico in the late 1960's, the park visitors could sign a register at the crater rim parking lot and leave their comments. Here are some of the more interesting, with an occasional remark by me in parentheses:

MALAPROPISMS AND MISSPELLINGS
Some visitors had the thought, but not the vocabulary
or spelling to express it:

"It is a huge whole."

"Scrupulous!"

"A truely experienced."

"Very natural."

"Kinda cool and windly."

"It is unique in its grossness."

"It would be more interesting if it errupted."

"What perrety rocks I saw."

"To a native anchiant & historical."

"Tote-Gote or burrow rentals."

"Pretty shocking - a nice place."

"Exuberating and enhancing."

"Should be better publizied."

"The magnificent view of the high plains was perspiring to see."

"Loved the trial." (They meant "trail")

"Like a minature modle of the Maies Vol."

"This is a good prospective for a science project." (I think they meant "prospect".)

"Very unique and breathlessly beautiful."

"Quite chillie."

"Chipmonks plentyful."

"Enthusing."

"Good seanry."

"Illustrative proof of internal forces of the earth."

"I like it beacuse it irrupted."

"Frightening."

"The geographical rock formations are very unusual."

"I taught it was suppurb."

"Fasinating and beutiful."

"Wonderful cenery."

"The scenery is so beautiful and exasperatin that it takes your breathe away."

"It's cold. I wasn't even tiresome."

"Good to have this a reserve of nature."

"Tiresome, but beautiful."

"Beautiful, artistic to draw."

HUMOR
Something about a public register brings out the funny side of quite a few visitors:

"What time does she blow?"

"When is the next eruption."

"Too bad it doesn't work."

"My fat wife couldn't make it."

"I'd like the cone better full of ice cream."

"I saw 3 deer and 2 girls." This was followed by "Saw the same 3 deer but the girls were gone."

"This would be a good place for mountain goat roping."

"I think I heard a rumble."

"Excellent for sacrifices."

"You think it won't blow again?"

"Wonderful...an air view without an airplane."

"Should give free nets and baskets to catch lizards."

"Is this where the Rolling Stones come from?"

"Better than the 70 cent spread."

"In the next Civil War the South will capture this place."

"Where is Lady Bird?" (Referring to Mrs. Johnson's activities in parks.)

"Look out for the lava...it burns."

"Very good except I ate a berry and found it was a ladybug."

"I'm gettin' dizzy as a boiled owl."

"So glad this happened long ago."

"Now that you got it what are you going to do with it?"

"We're on our honeymoon and WOW!"
This entry was followed by "We saw the people on their honeymoon and WOW!"

Mr. Bullington recalls hearing one visitor say, "It's the only one (volcano) in the United States."

COMPARISONS
There seems to be a universal desire to relate any scene to something from the visitors' previous experience:

"Corn is prettier and safer." (No doubt contributed by an Illinoisan or an Iowan.)

"No comparison to Colorado beauty."

"Oklahoma has some oil well blowouts but I guess this tops those."

"Almost as good Mt. Washington."

"Like Sunset Crater, except for colors."

"Reminds us of Point Rock near Elkhart."

"Comparable to Mt. Fuji in Japan."

"Got them bigger in Texas."

"Almost as pretty as Virginia"

"These were the rocks left over after they built Missouri."

"Nothing but rocks. We got rocks in Oklahoma."

"We ain't got nothing like this in Chicago."

"I prefer the Shenandoah Valley."

"Almost as interesting as Vesuvius in Italy."

"Almost as pretty as Dickens County."

"Something that Wichita doesn't have."

"This aint't nothin' like our big red hills."

"You should see the Andes Mountains."

Texas jokes were popular in this part of the country. Witness the following:

"Looks good after Texas."

"Only a Texas footprint."

"This hole must have been dug with a Texas shovel."

"What a Texas post hole."

"Texas ant hill."

"Texas doodle bug hole."

"Too bad it couldn't have been in Texas."

SCIENCE RELATED
Some visitors had questions about the natural history of the site, although it wasn't always obvious what they really meant:

"I want to know if a man was farming when the action occurred."

"Where are the bubbles?"

"Why don't you take up the poison so the animals can survive?"

"The moss seems greener on rocks."

"Why come those things are called 'bombs'?"

"Where's the big rock that melted?"

"Will it stay extinct?"

CRITICISMS
Obviously some folks weren't having a good time:

"Too high, but a great view."

"Trail is too smooth. We like it rough."

"It was a very tiring walk but I got through it."

"Needs more sights and could be a little more interesting but otherwise okay."

"Exhausting."

"Grubby and hard on the lungs."

"Wonderful, but in our excitement we locked a key in the car and will have to break a window to get in."

"Pityful."

"Very poor grade lava."

"I ain't from yesterday. I seen stuff like this before."

"Every time I look at it I feel like going to sleep."

Tourist Tip: When driving across South Dakota, stop in at Wall Drug and buy a copy of this book for a friend. Don't forget to see Mt. rushmore while you're there.

COMPLIMENTS
Other folks were enjoying themselves...I think:

"Your 15 cent folder made the trail unbelievably fascinating, awesome, and one of our most educational and interesting trips! (I hadn't realized that I was such a good writer.)

"Nature sure is marvelous."

"Perfect acoustics and perfect beauty."

"Very amusing."

"Ugh. But fun."

"We had nothing to do, so we came here, but is really interesting."

"A delightful surprise in terrain."

"Nice rangers you have here." (My personal favorite.)

"Dave Stimson is still the handsomest man in the National Park Service." (Obviously a personal friend of Superintendent S.)

"Very beautiful as far as I know."

"It was worth it I guess."

"Very interesting but very long."

And the ultimate accolade for a National Park Service area: "I like the comfort station."

PERCEPTIONS
The park had many repeat visitors, but they didn't all share the same ideas as to what they'd seen previously:

"It is prettier than in 1958."

"Hasn't changed much since 1956."

"Improved since our 1954 visit." (This was followed by "How do you improve a volcano?")

"Fixed up much better than in 1953."

"Looks quite different than it did 20 years ago (ca. 1947) when we were here."

"The trail seems so much steeper than it was 20 yrs. Ago."

"Quite a change since 1938."

"After our first visit 30 years ago (ca. 1937) it looks quite the same."

"Much improved since 1936."

"Looks much the same as in 1936."

CRATER RIM ROAD
More than a few visitors were unused to the steep
and narrow cinder road to the top of the mountain
and said as much in their comments:

"Eeek! I hope I find my stomach on the way back."

"Now to get back down."

"Nice, but I like flat land."

"Left my wife at the ranger station to knit."

"Very dangerous but nice."

"My wife helped me drive all the way up."

"Don't you provide blinders for scared husbands?"

"The drive scared my wife."

"Leaves you weak in the knees."

"Pretty high for a flat lander."

"If I ever get down I'll tell everyone about it."

"Scared the devils out of me."

"Scared to death of this place."

Not everyone felt that way, however:

"Road much improved. Much of the thrill of driving up is out."

POSTSCRIPT
Finally, one of the nicest things I can
remember reading in those registers:

"I dedicate this view to Jeanne,
the most beautiful girl in Texas."

****

Capulin Volcano is an example of a useless volcano. Some volcanoes contribute to the environment long after they've become extinct. Colorado's ancient San Juan Mountains are an example. They are the source of most of the sand that makes up the dunes tourists admire in southern Colorado's **Great Sand Dunes National Monument**. Southwest prevailing winds transport the sand from the floor of the San Luis Valley to a natural "trap" made by the Sangre De Cristo Mountains on the eastern side of the valley. A ranger continues:

With that in mind I was leading a dune walk one hot August day telling a group of middle school aged kids that "most of the sand that makes up the dunes originated in volcanoes." A young man raised his hand and asked, "Is that why the sand is so hot?"

Elegant flags, canyons and caves, petrified forests, explosive bats and extinct volcanoes, sand dunes — is that all the Southwest has to offer? No.

Mesa Verde National Park, Colorado's first national park, is a reminder that there are also a few cultural attractions in the Southwest. Established in 1906, the Park features the most notable and best preserved pre-Columbian cliff dwellings in the United States. Unfortunately, the Anasazi chose an inconvenient site for their community, as noted by Douglas Caldwell, presently a Public Information Officer at Rocky Mountain National Park.

> When I worked at Mesa Verde NP in the 1980s, we invariably would be asked, "Why did the Anasazi Indians build their 'ruins' (not villages) so far from the highway?" This reflected the visitor's impatience at having to drive more than 20 miles on a winding park road from the park entrance before reaching the area of the park where cliff dwellings are open to the public.

Another ranger submits the following item.

> I got this one from a woman whose name I don't recall, while attending a class at Harpers Ferry several years ago. She had worked at Mesa Verde for quite a while. Apparently while giving a tour of the ruins and talking about the life of the Native Americans who built the cliff dwellings, she would commonly talk about how, although primitive compared to our standards, these people actually had versions of amenities we have today, such as a certain plant that made a good toothbrush, one that was good as an aspirin, etc. One person on the tour was intrigued and asked, "Well, what did the Indians use in place of water?"

What an intriguing idea! Imagine the money that could be made if one could find a way to produce freeze-dried water!

****

I didn't know what to do with Utah. It's often classified as a Rocky Mountain state. Right — like mountain sheep and glaciers are a major impediment on the Utah salt flats where adrenaline junkies break all those speed records. "Don't get caught in an avalanche while swimming in Great Salt Lake kids!" "Perhaps I should write a separate chapter on the Great Basin," I thought. But I never received any Great Basin humor. Utah's premier icon, the honeybee, suggests Europe, but Europeans sent me no humorous material either. Utah's state flag allies it with the states east of the Missouri River. But Utah has more national parks and monuments than most of those states combined.

Then it struck me — nowhere have geological laws been more perverted than in Utah. Fortunately. Utah would be as bleak as South Dakota if it weren't for its ridiculous landscapes. In fact, Utah could be nicknamed the *Irrational State*. It is Utah's quirky landforms that give the nation some of its most inspired national parks and monuments — Zion, Bryce Canyon, Arches, Canyonlands, Rainbow Bridge; the very names conjure up visions of heaven, hell, Utah.

And where do these freakish landforms come from? The Colorado Plateau, the same elevated flattish area that covers so much of Arizona, New Mexico, and yes — even Colorado. That clinched it. Utah would become a part of the Southwest in my grand scheme.

I braced myself for an avalanche of canyon jokes and anecdotes about tourists lost in mazes and dead-end canyons. Instead, I received material relating to railroads and Abraham Lincoln. In fact, Utah might not even be included in this book if it weren't for Lincoln's assassination. I will try to rectify my mistake by featuring Utah next to Illinois — the *Land of Lincoln* — in my sequel.

****

Golden Spike National Historic Site commemorates the meeting of the Central Pacific and Union Pacific Railroads in 1869, completing the United States' first transcontinental railroad. The event was celebrated by the driving of a golden spike...at least, that's what I thought until I received the following letter.

The funniest things I ever heard visitors say was that the Golden Spike was driven in by famous characters like Abraham Lincoln and Brigham Young. It took me a while to convince the individual who thought . . . [Lincoln] drove in the Golden Spike that he was wrong. . . . I explained . . . that Lincoln had never been very far west of the Mississippi River and that he was assassinated in 1865 while the transcontinental railroad was completed in 1869. . . .

The truth is the Golden Spike was never driven in. You can imagine what would have happened if someone actually tried to do that. It was tapped into a pre-drilled hole (in the Laurel wood tie) by Central Pacific President Leland Stanford. There was also a Silver Spike, an Arizona Spike (made out of gold, iron and silver) and a 2nd Golden Spike. These also were tapped into the Laurel wood tie.

There was also a last iron spike.* The only difference between it and any other spike is that it was the last one to be driven in. A telegraph wire was tied around it so people could hear it being driven in from coast to coast.

Leland Stanford took a hearty swing and missed it. The crowd lost it and laughed out loud and hard. Stanford in great embarrassment handed the maul to Thomas Durant, Vice-President of the Union Pacific Railroad. Durant also humored the crowd by missing the spike.

Unlike Stanford, Durant was not embarrassed. He was sick when he attended the Golden Spike ceremony. He had just got stone drunk the night before, celebrating his release from kidnappers.

Thomas Durant was kidnapped by unpaid Union Pacific workers. He was being held in ransom for their promised wages. He was released when the Union Pacific coughed up the money.

Another funny fact about the history of the transcontinental railroad is that the UPRR and the CPRR over graded all the way across what is now Utah. It would have been funny enough if it had been an accident. This was done deliberately. The rival railroads were being paid in terms of land and money for all the grade they made. They used a lack of specific instruction to justify this ludicrous deed. The railroads however made no effort to notify the federal government about this situation. They just kind of let it be discovered. Furthermore they had the nerve to demand payment from the government for their over grading. Amazingly they were partially paid for this nonsense.

*There's an idea for a NPS unit — Last Iron Spike National Historic Site.

Sadly, Utah doesn't advertise its quirkiness and natural beauty on its state flag. Rather, the banner is as rational — and therefore as dull — as any state flag, depicting a bald eagle, two national flags, and a beehive against a blue background. "What manner of state is it that hosts bald eagles and whose residents raise honeybees and fly United States national flags? Let's visit this exotic wonderland called Utah!"

As Utah's Statehood Centennial (1996) approaches, I would like to present my design for a Utah state flag (Above). It is distinctive, symbolically appropriate, and perhaps even attractive and therefore eminently irrational as state flags go.

My design retains the *Beehive State*'s beehive, a Mormon symbol. (Like most Utahans, honeybees originated in Europe.) Superimposed on the brown beehive is a golden arrowhead commemorating Utah's original inhabitants, particularly the Utes for which Utah is named. The beehive and arrowhead combined suggest *multiculturalism*, a radical, almost heretical concept among state flags. This would further showcase Utah's irrationality.

The white background and thin blue stripes represent the snows and waters of the Rocky Mountains, peace, and serenity. White is also the color of the California gull and sego lily, Utah's state bird and flower. Thicker red stripes at top and bottom represent the Colorado Plateau, the yellow geometric designs they encompass the canyons that have been carved out of it. (Vexillologist Jefferey Flohr suggests replacing the latter with a Native American design.)

(Top) Unlike today's generation, which has been spoiled and perverted by a mild climate, abundance, beautiful beaches, Hollywood, and Disneyland, early Californians were eminently practical. Why build a road around a tree when you could just bore a hole through it? Of course, there was less bureaucracy to deal with back then. Today, you would have to file an environmental impact statement before you could tunnel through a redwood.

(Bottom) When Dakotans heard there were trees that could be driven through, they hurried west to see them.

CALIFORNIA
The Golden (Eagle Pass) State

California merits a chapter all by itself. California's geographic diversity can be illustrated by the fact that the lowest elevation in the Western Hemisphere — in Death Valley — is a mere 80 air miles from Mt. Whitney, the highest point in the Lower 48 States. California's biodiversity is attested to by its redwoods — Earth's largest living organisms — which are supported by soil that is infested with organisms so small one needs a microscope to see them.

Remarkably diverse themselves, Californians are known for their free-spirited ways. Surfing, channeling, Hollywood, Silicon Valley — these are images conjured up by mere mention of the *Golden State*. Californians gave the nation its first official state insect and reptile. Both were signed into law by Governor Ronald Reagan, a cowboy who might have been considered an alien in the Dakotas.

California's wildest wilderness may be the urban wilderness of Los Angeles. Fronting on the sandy beaches north of Los Angeles, **Santa Monica National Recreation Area** receives plenty of visitors. A Park Ranger sent me plenty of material.

The Santa Monica Mountains National Recreation Area visitor center provides information for all National Parks and we get thousands of phone calls weekly.* Most of the calls are intelligent questions that can be answered rather quickly and informatively. Occasionally we do get some rather interesting questions. . . .

Other questions that have been received in the visitor center over the years have been, "Where can we go camp and live on love?" and "Where is Golden Eagle Pass?"** At our site dedicated to filming and filming history Paramount Ranch, often while a television show or movie is being filmed the ranger on duty is asked if she is "Real." Another is for the visitor to come up to a ranger in full uniform and ask "Do you work here?"

*Author's note: I list this contributor's first contribution under Yosemite.

**A Golden Eagle Pass allows the bearer and occupants of the bearer's vehicle free access to any national park, monument, or wildlife refuge that normally charges a fee. Anyone under age 62 can purchase a Golden Eagle Pass for $25.

When Santa Monica Mountains first acquired Cheeseboro canyon the neighboring properties ran cattle and often the cattle would jump the fence and enter . . . the park to graze. In the summer of 1986 a large herd of sixty or so cattle trespassed into Cheeseboro Canyon. One of the patrol rangers called in to help round up the cattle was a city boy . . . [who] knew nothing about cattle. He decided that the best way to round up the cattle was to drive at the cattle as fast as possible in his four wheel drive with the siren blasting away. Needless to say he learned a quick lesson about startled and scared cattle. They spread out in every direction at a full run. It took days to find all the cattle again.

My informant adds that a pet cow was lost in Cheeseboro Canyon in 1994. Cows aren't the only creatures that get lost in California.

****

Come to the woods, for here is rest. There is no repose like that of the green deep woods. Here grow the wall-flower and the violet. The squirrel will come and sit upon your knee, the log-cock will wake you in the morning. Sleep in the forgetfulness of all ill. Of all the upness accessible to mortals, there is no upness comparable to the mountains.

If these words sound like the ravings of a lunatic lost in the wilderness, they are. But the author was no ordinary lunatic — he was John Muir. His divorce from reality was confirmed by Henry Fairfield Osborn who noted in his *Impressions of Great Naturalists* that Muir "wrote about trees as no one else in the whole history of trees, chiefly because he loved them as he loved men and women."

More than a dreamer, Muir acted out his fantasies. In 1874, he was hiking in the Sierras of northern California with his favorite companion — himself — in December. While most people were working or inside keeping warm, Muir found himself in the midst of a winter storm. Like a simpleton just awakened by a log-cock, the confused Muir climbed high up a Douglas fir and hung on for the ride of his eccentric life.* His arboreal perch presumably kept him safe from hungry bears that might have been roused from hibernation by the storm.

---

*Perhaps Muir, who had emigrated from Scotland, felt some kinship with the Douglas fir, which was discovered by another Scotsman, David Douglas.

Like a pioneer *Forrest Gump*, Muir once walked 1,000 miles from Indiana to the Gulf of Mexico. He might have sought his fortune in the Gulf Coast shrimp fishery or recited poetry to pelicans, but Muir bounced on to California. He spent six years in Yosemite, where he was the first to demonstrate that the spectacular valley was formed by glacial erosion. (How Muir demonstrated this is not recorded; presumably he painted himself white and crawled across the valley, digging up rocks and boulders as astonished Native Americans gazed in awe. Perhaps that is why Native Americans put up so little resistance to white invaders in California; they thought they were dealing with a race of medicine men.) Having contributed to the American dream with his exciting news about glaciers, Muir went to Alaska and discovered his very own glacier nursery, Glacier Bay. Why he didn't demonstrate how enormous chunks of ice fall off tidewater glaciers into the sea is a mystery only Muir can answer.

If Muir had lived during the Ice Age, he might have become the *Supreme Eco-Commander* of Planet Earth. If Muir had lived in the Dakotas, he would have been roped and branded for the entertainment of tourists. But in 19th-century California Muir merely attracted like-minded kooks and squirrels. His cult earned official status in 1892 as the Sierra Club. The Sierra Club continues to campaign vigorously for the preservation of wilderness so that members shod for Himalayan climbing expeditions can invade the wilderness in mass outings. In quest of solitude and spirituality, these environmental warriors trample endangered alpine plants into oblivion as they jostle for space in which to scoop water out of streams with their quaint metal "Sierra cups" and pour it over freeze-dried meals that could be served in four-star restaurants — and probably are in California.

Though he might sound dangerous, Muir was a harmless kook. Indeed, he was as beneficial as the diverse funguses that grow in Pacific Northwest forests. After spending ten years in California growing — you guessed it, fruit — Muir earned enough money to dedicate his life to conservation. (One can only wonder what Muir might have unleashed on the world if he had followed his other passion, inventing — Portable igloos? Escalators for squirrels and log-cocks? Arboreal basements?) Muir's efforts were instrumental in the passage of the Yosemite National Park bill in 1890, creating Yosemite and Sequoia national parks.

This man who wouldn't harm a squirrel if it ran off with his favorite tree signed a devil's pact with one of the century's greatest mass murderers — Theodore Roosevelt. Muir persuaded Roosevelt to set aside 148 million acres of forest reserves, sufficient to raise squirrels for Roosevelt to shoot at and Muir to talk to, with a few left over for other Americans to enjoy.

Thousands of seabirds known as murres and murrelets wander aimlessly about the North Pacific. The aberrant marbled murrelet, nests in enormous coastal conifers, where the supply of fish can never be diminished. A bird-brained seabird that sits high in fog-drenched conifers daydreaming about Glacier Bay might be imagined to be the reincarnation of John Muir. Perhaps one of them is.

The two things Muir loved most — glaciers and trees — are commemorated by Alaska's Muir Glacier and California's **Muir Woods National Monument**. The latter is a leader in arboreal humor, as the following items indicate.

As a first year seasonal at Muir Woods in 1975, I was in awe of the coast redwoods, as well as John Muir, the man the monument was dedicated to. While walking down a path, I found myself following a few paces behind two fellows, one apparently a local and the other a guest. I overheard the guest ask his friend, "So who was this John Muir guy, anyway?" In my mind, I was already reciting the many and great accomplishments of this renowned naturalist, as if he had asked me, when I heard the local resident reply, "Oh, he was some old guy with a hotdog stand a little way up the trail."

Many parks have a question or two that seem to be on the lips of every other visitor. At Muir Woods the question was, and is, "Where's the Drive-through tree?" referring to one of a few trees that roads had been cut through such as the giant sequoia in Yosemite that had fallen. Although there had never been a tree with a hole cut in it for a car to drive through in Muir Woods, every ranger heard this question so frequently that the answer came out almost before the question was finished. This was the case, around 1976, when a woman asked another ranger and I "Where is the *see-through* tree?" I had to catch myself from giving the usual answer while I tried to determine if she meant the drive-through tree, but my coworker responded immediately with "Well, it's right here. Can't you see it?" as he ran his hand down the bark of an imaginary redwood tree.

On another occasion, a rather impatient young man asked the "drive-through tree question" and didn't really like the standard answer, and repeated, "Yeah, but where is the one here?" The ranger, deciding a turn in strategy was required, answered, "Well, you can drive through any tree if you can get up enough speed; it's a simple law of physics."

Disturbingly, on more than one occasion, visitors emerged from a walk through Muir Woods asking, "Now where are the redwoods?" I can only presume they meant the other, or giant, sequoia since when I tried to explain they had just walked through a redwood forest, and the difference between the two types of redwoods in California, they still seemed not to have a clue.

Incidentally, California recognizes two California redwoods as official state trees. Coast redwood and redwood are common names for *Sequoia sempervirens*, while giant sequoia, bigtree, and Sierra redwood identify *Sequoiadendron giganteum*.

The tallest known coast redwood is 364 feet high. The State of California and the Save-the-Redwoods League matched monies to protect coast redwoods, which are sheltered in designated groves.

Enormous giant sequoias occur in thirty-two groves on the western slopes of the Sierra Nevada mountains. A sequoia nicknamed "General Sherman" is estimated to be 3,000 to 4,000 years old. At 36½ feet in diameter, it is the largest living organism on Earth and perhaps in the solar system. It is estimated that General Sherman could supply enough lumber to build forty houses.

If John Muir hadn't been such a tree nut, he could have toppled General Sherman, built 40 houses, and sold them. He would then have had enough money to take a few hundred squirrels with him to Antarctica, which is essentially one big glacier. Fortunately, Muir spared General Sherman and helped preserve a national park that was carved by glaciers to boot.

His hot dog stand a failure, John Muir tried to make a living as a guide. He specialized in glacier walks, squirrel talks, and glass-bottom boat tours through redwood forests. In the above photo, Muir is sitting in a glass-bottom boat, hidden behind an enormous see-through redwood. Sadly, most giant see-through redwoods — including the famed "General Custer" tree pictured above — were harvested for use in making windows. Today, see-through redwoods are a prime target for timber poachers, as their lumber can be easily smuggled past rangers. One can only wonder if future generations of Americans will have an opportunity to not see such wonders of Nature.

Some Californians tout **Yosemite** as the first **National Park**. Abraham Lincoln signed legislation protecting Yosemite Valley and Mariposa Big Tree Grove on June 30, 1864, before President Grant established Yellowstone as a national park. First or second, Yosemite ranks among the most scenic of national parks. Giant redwoods and spectacular crowds of visitors dominate the lowlands, which are battered by the nation's highest waterfalls. With the Greenhouse Effect, one must wonder whether these waterfalls and Yosemite's most famous attractions — the sheer granite faces that challenge the world's top climbers — will always be with us.

The following item was contributed by a ranger at Santa Monica Mountains National Recreation Area.

In 1987, Yosemite National Park had dozens of fires burning within it which had made the newspapers. Our visitor center [Santa Monica Mountains National Recreation Area] received a call from a concerned citizen who asked whether Half Dome had melted in the fires. When he was told that half dome had not melted because it is made of granite, the caller explained that he had heard that Yosemite was a Glacier Valley and thought that everything was made of ice.

Another correspondent said the most humorous question he had entertained during his 28 years as a ranger or superintendent was asked in Yosemite.

I was a park ranger working in the Mariposa Grove of redwoods in the spring of 1969, following the winter in which the Wawona Tree (famous redwood tree with a road tunnel cut through it) fell down as a result of heavy snow and winter storms. A middle-aged couple, having discovered that the Wawona Tree had fallen asked, "Will you put the dead tree back up?"

Still another correspondent reminds us that Yosemite offers more than melting rocks and temporarily disabled giant redwoods.

Bears were very much a part of the park ranger's daily experience during my years at Yellowstone and Yosemite, and somewhat at Crater Lake. The bear stories were many and some humorous. In 1969 and 1971 I worked the Valley District and bear problems in the campgrounds were frequent. Black bears which became a nuisance or a threat to campers were trapped, tagged and relocated outside the valley. If the bear returned to the Valley and continued being a problem, especially a third time, it was shot with a drug overdose to kill it and transported away in a culvert trap.

The humorous aspect of this is the dead bear dumping. The bear would be transported at night out on the Crane Flat road north of the Valley where the road is carved out of the side of the cliff and the mountain is precipitous. At a certain milepost stake where the rock slope from the road was almost vertical, the bear transporting detail would stop and drop the dead bear over the edge of the road and down the cliff.

This occurred for a number of years and sometimes I would be amused with the thought that in 50 or more years, when a biologist is searching out the great secrets of animal behavior and exploring the cliff base under the place where dozens of dead bears were dumped, a huge pile of bear bones would be found. Not knowing that rangers 50 years ago dropped dead bears from the cliffs above, the biologist would certainly think a major discovery had occurred.

Here, it would be speculated, came bears from miles around, driven by an inherent sense of the approach of death, retreating to this 'Cliff of the Bones' to die amongst the spirits of its ancestors. With this new found evidence previously unknown to the scientific world, a new animal behavioral theory is advanced and Yosemite contributes again to the vast storehouse of scientific knowledge.*

****

Except for a noticeable decrease in vegetation and increase in temperature, Southern California's Death Valley is really not that different from the *Golden State*'s coastal redwood forests. That **Death Valley National Park** includes the lowest point in the Western Hemisphere is all the more remarkable when one considers that the highest point in the Lower 48 States is California's 14,495-foot Mt. Whitney, which stands a mere 80 air miles or 152 driving miles away. Death Valley is famous for its heat and aridity, which were not sufficient to deter early miners from exploring for gold and borax. I received an unusually entertaining story about Death Valley from a Park Ranger.

---

*Are you listening, Hollywood? *Bear Stampede* could be a really exciting movie!

Here in Death Valley, as you can imagine, there have been numerous stories relating to death. In the late 1800's there were stories circulating that somewhere out here there was a fountain of scalding blood. There was supposed to be a poison gas that issued forth from the rocks out here to kill people. There were demons that wandered around under the direction of the devil. Some theologians thought that this was the roof of the Biblical hell and you could hear the wails of the damned crying out from below. Another theologian theorized that this had been Eden and it was torn and accursed because of the shameful conduct that had taken place here.

One of the stories about Death Valley was the story about the salvation of the area from poison gas. This story appeared in newspapers in 1890 and it concerned Colonel John Jewks who came into the valley on stilts to get rid of the poison gas. In his pockets he had little gophers that he would drop on the ground and then register the gas on his gasometer as it choked the life out of the gophers. When he got to the center of the Valley, he saw a sight that made his hair stand on end.

Down far below him there was a huge group of wagons, dead animals and dead people, all drowned in a sea of deadly gas. However on looking at the scene more closely, he observed sparkling piles that looked liked silver and gold. The Colonel just had to figure out how to get to that silver and gold without himself dying from the gas. So he sat on a hill and thought and thought and he came up with the idea of lighting a huge fire and dropping it down into the valley thereby causing the gas to explode.

The plan worked perfectly. The gas exploded, turning the Colonel's hair white and barbecuing the buzzards that hovered overhead.* As the Colonel was going back down to fetch the silver and gold that would make his fortune, he discovered that the explosion had worked so well that it not only got rid of the poison gas but it had also vaporized the wagons, dead animals, dead people and the piles of silver and gold.

This story is related in a number of publications about Death Valley including the Richard Lingenfelter book, *Death Valley and the Amargosa*.

Of course everyone in Death Valley is thrilled to be able to say that we were made a park on Halloween and will now celebrate our anniversary every year on that day.

---

*Author's Note: When I read about a white-haired Colonel and barbecued buzzards, I suspected that I was reading the mythical account of the origin of Kentucky Fried Chicken. How stupid of me! Colonel Sanders is from the South, I think, and Kentucky Fried Chicken is not sold in Death Valley, as far as I know.

****

Caught up in the excitement of giant redwoods, melting glacial valleys, Death Valley, and the urban wildlife that migrate through them, many visitors forget all about California's biggest habitat — the sea. To remind Californians that the waves they surf on are products of the sea, the federal government established a national park in that sea.

Channel Islands National Park consists of five islands off southern California: Anacapa, San Miguel, Santa Barbara, Santa Cruz, and Santa Rosa. The islands are known for their nesting sea birds, sea lion rookeries, and unique terrestrial species. During the Pleistocene, or Ice Age, the islands were surrounded by water and were inhabited by a pygmy mammoth (not to be confused with a mammoth pygmy).

Mark Connally, an employee of Island Packers, a company that has been "cruising the islands for education, recreation and research since 1968," sent me the following list of "FAVORITE QUESTIONS AT CHANNEL ISLANDS NATIONAL PARK CONCESSIONERS OFFICE OF ISLAND PACKERS":

When does the 9:00 boat leave?

Does the island go all the way to the bottom?

Why do the birds only sit on the white rocks?

Do you do whale watching at night?

These are but an appetizer, the main course being a compilation of questions and quips Channel Islands National Park's staff have compiled over the years. They've even given this amalgamation a title: *Real Questions...Actual questions uttered from the mouths of CHIS N.P. visitors, having absolutely NOTHING to do with the Channel Islands OR Questions asked where you're dying to respond (politely) "How in the hell should I know?"* I'm told this treasury of Channel Islands wit is on display in the Visitors Center. The following excerpts have been reorganized, with names and dates deleted.

After reading the following questions and comments, readers may be inspired to lobby Congress to give Park Rangers a raise. People who can answer questions like these deserve annual salaries of at least $45,000.

The photograph above was taken by Jack Couffer and appears in his book *Bat Bomb* with the following caption: "Pearl Harbor Day, Santa Rosa Island. Fletch excavating jaw of a pygmy elephant. A short time later, cowboys told us we were at war." If you read the chapter on the Southwest, then you've already had a bellyful of *Bat Bomb*. One of the greatest contributors of material for *(IR)Rational Parks* was an anonymous donor from the USS *Arizona* Memorial, which commemorates Japan's attack on Pearl Harbor. The *biggest* contributor of material was an anonymous donor from Channel Islands (CHIS) National Park, which is where the above photo was taken. As if this is not coincidence enough, the cowboys are reminders of my native South Dakota. And get this — a pygmy mammoth skeleton discovered in CHIS in 1994 was sent to the Mammoth Site in Hot Springs, South Dakota! All things are truly connected!

IDENTITY CRISIS!

"Is this a gift shop?"
No — this is the headquarters for Channel Islands National Park.
"Oh...bummer"

Channel Islands National Park
"This isn't the Nestle Chocolate Company?"
No — this is Channel Islands National Park
"Are you sure?"
Yes
"This isn't 471-6184?"
No
"Isn't that funny?"
Hilarious, Mam

2 minutes later:
Channel Islands National Park
"This isn't 471-6184?"
No mam
"This isn't the Nestle Chocolate Company?"
No mam
"Isn't this funny? Isn't this the funniest thing?"
Not really mam

(Chocolate, or wilderness — continued in next column)

1 minute later:
Channel Islands National Park
"I could swear this is 471-6184. I could swear this is the Nestle Chocolate Company."
Me — maybe it's time to get the operator in on this. Maybe she could help you.
"OK — could you give me her number?"

CHIS Nat'l Park, can I help you?
"This isn't K-Mart?"
No mam it isn't.
"Are you sure?"
Give me a break!!

Is this the place where a boat is on its side in the water? And if not where is it? And how do I get there? How does a person get out to the Islands? If this is called a national park, where is the park so we can have a picnic?

Is the mission open tomorrow after church services for people to just look around? I just thought you might know 'cause maybe it's in your department.

MYSTERIOUS NATURALPHENOMENA

Little girl looking into the tidepool:
"Wow, there's real water in there!"

"What is that purple in the tidepool?"
It was the reflection from his wife's blouse!

HISTORY

How did Rincon get its name? Is it a Chumash word?

Where did that fleet of destroyers go down in the 1940's? Show me on this map.

Who built the monument?

HERSTORY
Woman explaining mortars to her child: The Indians used these to grind corn, you see, and then they made tortillas.

FLORA & FAUNA

As we were driving in I saw those trees about this tall. [motioned shoulder height] What were they?!

"What's that grass?"
Excuse me lady — Could you at least <u>point</u> in a <u>general direction</u>!?!

Do whales eat people?

Doesn't this baleen grow on the bottom of the ocean and then whales pick it up & put it in their mouths?

"Do you have dolphins here?"
Yes, in the water.
"Where is the aquarium?"

"Hey (Man) — Like a friend of mine just told me (man) that he heard that there's a herd (man) of 25 Great White Sharks comin' down from like Monterey. Like he just heard it on the radio (man). Like should I go surfing tomorrow or not (man)?"
Yes. Go surfing & let's hope the story is true...

"I just got my period & I'm concerned about sharks. Where we come from they are everywhere & I love to swim. Is it ok?"
No problem. No worries, the biggest you'll see is a horn shark. About 1 ½ ft.
"Oh good, I feel much better."
(Next day's newspaper) — Great white spotted off SCI — I wonder if she'll trust a Park Ranger again...

How many times have people been bitten by sharks up here?

Lady pointing to the shark egg case: These are crabs — you know the crabs live in these.

What are those fish swimming around the dock? They are big & have fins.

What are those big fish I see up north?

I'm trying to tell my girlfriend about the fish I saw in Okinawa — they are yellow and blue and really mean looking. What are they?

What is that colorful fish that starts with O? I saw it in my crossword puzzle.

A visitor asked the name of a fish — when we told her "Sarcastot Fringehead" she said "I have a brother-in-law like that!!"

Visitor looking at strings of sea hare eggs: "Who dropped their noodles in the tank?"

What do you call a sand dollar before it's one of these dead sand dollars you find on the beach? **possible response (a baby sand dollar?!) OR a sand fifty-cent piece??**

(Asked by boy about four years old): "What's that purple one?"
A bat star.
"(Shriek!) Does it fly?"

Why don't the piers and rocks here at the Ventura harbor have mussels on them? The piers and rocks at the Channel Islands Harbor does.

Kid . . .How much do the crabs cost?

(FLORA & FAUNA — Continued on page 173)

LOCAL ATTRACTIONS & WEATHER

"I need the weather for Zion National Park. We're heading for Arizona to see it today."
1) I don't know the weather in Arizona.
2) Zion Nat'l Park is in Utah, not Arizona you blithering idiot.
3) Get a clue.

Do you know a good place to eat in San Francisco?

Where are the party fishing boats?

Where can we board the Aloha?

Is the mission at Punta Baja open on Thanksgiving Day? It's a national park, near Point Conception!

Where's the best place to buy a skateboard?

"Hi! Could you tell me about weather conditions today at the Grand Canyon?"
Nope. Fraid I can't.
"Oh... you mean you haven't talked to them today?"
Puh-leez!

"Do you know who I can call to get a permit to go down the Colorado River near Havasu?"

"What is the phone number for Cider Grove?"

Wrong Park!!

Can you tell me about the crowd conditions in Yosemite during the holiday season?

I need information on Hearst Castle — give me all you have.

"Where's the Lounge?"
The bathroom? It's right over there across the breezeway.
"No, the LOUNGE — you know — THE BAR! I'm supposed to meet someone at the Channel Islands Harbor Lounge."
Well, this ain't it but go take a drink in the tide pool, buddy

How do you get to that little fishing village near Rubio's?

Is there a bridge out to the islands or what?! I saw a sign that said 5 miles to the Channel Islands but I turned right and came here instead.

Do you have a map of piles of sand underwater?

Could you tell me about that aquarium in Monterey?

What's there to see in Harbortown?

Do you know anything about the new Museum in LaJolla?

Are there restaurants on the Ventura pier? (I'm sure — winter)

TRIVIA QUIZ

What is the world's safest beach?

Where are all the land faults in southern California?

What's the average cost to dock a boat in Southern California?

How high is Morro Rock in Sequoia?

CHALLENGING DIRECTIONS

How do I get to the snow from Buellton? I can see it from my house.

Where are islands around here?

(Letter): Please send me the addresses of the islands of CHIS.

Her: What is the fastest way to walk back to the Harbor Town Hotel?
Me: Walk back down Spinnaker (pointing)
Her: You mean I can't walk behind this way (pointing)
Me: No, that is the entrance of the harbor and there is no bridge.
Her: You mean I can't walk behind this way (pointing)
Me: No, that is the entrance of the harbor and there is no bridge (Didn't we just go thru this?)
Her: Well, they must of changed things because you used to be able to do it.
Me: ???

How can I get to the tunnel or bridge across to the islands?

LOST AND FOUND

I'm looking for a couple of ladies — have you seen them?

"Do you know where my husband is?"
No I don't. (Who the hell is your husband? Lady there are about 50 people in the building and I don't even know what your husband looks like!)

"Where am I?"

RANGERS ARE INTERESTING, TOO

Do you people really need degrees to work here?

I heard you say you're a SCUBA diver. I didn't know women could do that. Are you sure they can?

Boy: How come you have curly hair?
Me: Speechless.

RANGERS' TURN

(School group) Have any of you visited a National Park? Which one? "Disneyland!"

FLORA & FAUNA
(Continued from page 171)

"We're moving to Ventura County and we hear there are mountain lions. Is that so?"
Suggested Forest Service!

How do I train my canary to sit on my finger?

Young visitor, after seeing stuffed redtail: Do you have The Eagle here?

Why have the squirrel numbers been reduced? — I know because I used to raise squirrels...

Is that an elephant bone in the corner? (Author's note: Maybe it was! Diminutive elephants inhabited islands around the world. North America's representative was the Channel Islands' pygmy mammoth (*Mammuthus exilis*). It was known mostly from scattered bones until a sensational specimen was discovered on Santa Rosa Island in June, 1994.)

BEYOND THE CALL OF DUTY
At $45,000 a year, people who can answer questions like these are a bargain!

I hear being a ranger on the islands is lonely & depressing & I want to work there... I also hear they make $45,000 a year!

Visitor (with about 15 people wandering around in the VC, me putting up an exhibit, 2:30 pm): Are you open?

"Hello? Yes... Is this a government office?"

Yes sir — it's Channel Islands National Park.

"Where and when can I buy government bonds or oxims for such?"

WHAT'S AN OXIM?!!

Where can I call to save the wild burros from getting shot?

Where can I get information on getting U.S. citizenship?

Can you translate this brochure into German?

Post card received from Poland:

BITTE FORDERN SIE BEI BEDARE DIE ENTSRRELHENDEN UNTBALGEN AN

A woman from someplace in Alaska called. She said she had a plastic molding of an Admiral Bird and wanted to know where she could get the chest of the molding fixed?? Geeze Louise!!

Can I burn juniper wood in my fireplace?

Phone Call: Why is SMI closed on some days? Why can't I bring my dog? We boaters hate the National Park. Why isn't a ranger available to pick up after my dog?

In the parking lot... "My phone's not working. You're here to fix it — right?"

No — I'm a PARK RANGER you idiot!

If I get married on a boat off Santa Cruz Island would it be legal? Or should I come back to Ventura to get it legalized?

I just invented something. Could you please issue me a patent?

Man on phone: In Morro Bay, I saw a product called "Jack's Itching Remedy," with a Forest Service letter attached attesting to its quality. Do you know where I can get some?

On the credit card phone: How much do you charge for a car wax?

Do you know what the scope of utilities is in the British Honduras or Belize?

HUH?

Hi — do you know anything about who to call about trash pickup at our home?

moved here from New York. What's going on?"

Do you know how to forward mail to my brother? I don't know where he moved to, but I'm getting his child support bills, phone bills and other letters.

Today's mail asked us to assist in finding a large house with eight to eleven bedrooms suitable for a family reunion. Suggested C of C!!

The Civil Service was ruined forever when they let the Post Office in. But I guess you know that.

Him: Why is the flag at half mast?
Me: To honor Congressman Leland who died in a plane crash in Ethiopia.
Him: That really makes me angry. Why should he get special treatment — you wouldn't lower the flag for me if I got hit by a truck.
Me: (I wish!) Well, he was an important Congressman and the federal government wanted to show respect for him.
Him: Well, I think it's wrong. I'm not going to hold you responsible but I want you to know I don't agree.
Me: (Are you going to arrest me or what?!) Well, write to your congressman. (I-yi yi!)

The mail today yielded this: "Please send me information regarding the American Galapagos islands. I read about them in Buzzworm magazine."

My son wants to go to Santa Cruz College. How will you get him on & off the island? I want to make sure he'll be home for Christmas.

A Visitor asked if there was a stagecoach stop on Santa Rosa Island.

When are they going to fix the pier?

Oh, I've seen the movie already — isn't it the same one you show down at Cabrillo Monument?

Can you sell me a bus ticket? I want to ride a bus through the Channel Islands.

Do you have to be a certain height to ride the boat?

Could you give me the paddle boat regulations?

From a woman who must've been at least 173 years old: I used to have a house at the corner of 5th and Harbor. What did you do with it?

"Where are the Russian ships? The newspaper said the ships were here?"
I don't know. This question has been asked for two weeks.

Where can I dump out my bathroom tanks from my motor home?

Why can't you drink the water on Anacapa?

Why can't I target shoot near the islands?

"Who takes care of the arch?"
Me: It is a naturally occurring phenomenon — nobody takes care of it. (Who takes care of you?)

Where can I kennel my cat?

"Here's my camera. I'm sure you'll want it while I look around in here."

Hey — thanks!
Nice Nikon.

"Where should I put the jack-a-lope picture?" I thought — "under THE DAKOTAS or in the article on Cervid Metamorphosis in the Appendix?" Then I read the material from Channel Islands National Park and knew exactly where it belongs. With wings spread, tail upraised, and antlers locked into position, this jack-a-lope is in attack mode.

THE PACIFIC NORTHWEST
Towering Trees and Giant Fleas

Few regions loom larger in Americans' imagination than the Pacific Northwest. Here snow-capped volcanoes challenge the sky, salty waves pound against rugged wilderness beaches, and grasslands flourish atop ancient lava flows as vast as the national deficit.

But the Pacific Northwest is best known for its vast forests of often immense trees. That these evergreen monarchs survive is something Americans should give thanks for. During World War II, when members of Project-X were experimenting with the use of bats as carriers of incendiary devices, some people worried that the Japanese might be up to the same trick. In his book *Bat Bomb*, Jack Couffer reprints the following note.

> I talked with Dr. Adams and am not certain he doesn't have something. A few hundred thousand bats so equipped if released at many places from a sub along our Pacific coast might very well cause so many forest fires that an almost total loss of timber would occur.

Fortunately, the Japanese had no Carlsbad Caverns or similar bat incubators. As Couffer relates, they were undaunted.

> The Japanese weren't considering using bat bombs, of that we can now be sure, but by odd coincidence they would later use another method nearly as ingenious to achieve the same result. By sending unmanned incendiary balloons borne by the prevailing winds from Japan eastward across the Pacific they aimed to incinerate our Pacific Northwest forests. Although several balloons made the long crossing on their own and fires were ignited, the effectiveness of the effort was practically nil.

Where the Japanese failed, Americans succeeded spectacularly. "To hell with balloons, we'll use chain saws!" There are wilderness preserves where forest patriarchs still stretch skyward, taunting foreign terrorists and America's timber industry alike — "Come and get us!" In recent years, wolves and grizzly bears — long ago exterminated in Washington and Oregon — have been cautiously exploring northern Washington from their Canadian sanctuary. If they hurry up, there may be a few big trees left for them to see.

Plants and animals aren't the only endangered natural phenomena in the Pacific Northwest. The region's famed volcanoes have a habit of disappearing as well. Fortunately, **Mt. Rainier National Park**'s namesake is still with us. At 14,410 feet, Mount Rainier is the highest mountain in Mt. Rainier National Park and one of the highest in the Lower 48. It also spawns the greatest array of glaciers south of Canada. During the summer, guides employed by Rainier Mountaineering lead a virtual assembly line of climbers to Rainier's summit, which can be reached merely by walking.* More ambitious climbers seek out more strenuous routes on the glaciers and snowfields that have trained many an expedition bound for the Himalayas.

Mt. Rainier boasts the world record for snowfall, making one wonder why it isn't called Mt. Snowier. The name Rainier commemorates an early explorer, rather than atmospheric phenomena however. As a proper wilderness preserve, it is underdeveloped, as one ranger came to appreciate.

> On a beautiful summer day at Mt. Rainier, I was collecting fees at the park's entrance station when three twenty-year olds drive up and ask, "Is there a mall up here?" (Sorry, we only have one of the most magnificent mountains in the U.S., wildflowers, hiking trails, wildlife, etc. — but maybe it's about time the park had a REAL attraction — a MALL!)**

Mt. St. Helens National Volcanic Monument is administered by the USDA Forest Service. A ranger advises me that "When do the deer turn into elk?" is a common question there. She also recalls a visitor who informed her that she had seen a mountain lion. "Oh really, can you describe it?" the ranger queried. "It was this big," the visitor responded, as her hands framed an invisible object about the size of a housecat, "and black."

Of course, Mt. St. Helens is not known so much for its black, housecat-sized mountain lions as it is for something else it's missing — part of Mt. St. Helens. Before Mt. St. Helens erupted, it was arguably the most beautiful mountain in the Cascades. If it takes a disaster to

---

*These same guides lead them back down.

**The National Park Service administers a National Mall. Appropriately, it's in Washington, D.C.

get the National Park Service and USDA Forest Service's attention, why don't they confer monument status on sites that have been devastated by earthquakes, blizzards, or severe infestations of insect pests? How about an LA Riot National Recreation Area?

The answer is simple: The paying public simply would not pay to camp in a Fungal Rot National Park, a Gypsy Moth National Forest, or a Car-Jacking Cultural Site that offers demonstrations. Wisely, the National Park Service and USDA Forest Service have invested our tax dollars in volcanoes.

One of the best known volcanic units in the system is Oregon's **Crater Lake National Park**. About 7,700 years ago, Mt. Mazama blew its top. The resultant caldera filled with water. Today, Crater Lake is renowned for its deep blue color. At a depth of 1,932 feet, the lake is the United States' deepest.

Mazama is a Spanish word that has been applied to a number of animals, including the mountain goat. Any mountain goats that may have once lived on Mazama's slopes were probably deposited in Montana. (The mountain goat is an unofficial symbol of Montana's Glacier National Park.)

A ranger sends the following Crater Lake questions:

Does the lake go all the way around?

Is it as far up as it is down?

How do I get to the bottom of the lake?

Do I go out the same way I came in?

What is that plant outside with the green leaves?

Another park ranger contributed this tidbit.

As a naturalist at Crater Lake, I was presenting a talk on the lake's formation when I was asked "Is Wizard Island a floating island?"

Islands don't float, of course. However, some rocks of volcanic origin do float. Such rocks are riddled with cavities, making them exceptionally light. Also, there is a Bogoslof Island in Alaska's Aleutian Islands that might give the appearance of floating. It is simply an active underwater volcano whose intermittent activity has caused it to break the surface at slightly different locations.

Another correspondent offers a musical selection from Crater Lake.

Humor in the national parks appears in many forms including songs. . . . At Crater Lake in the early 1970s (and maybe even today) the ranger presenting the evening campground program at the Mazama campground led the campers in a humorous song about Crater Lake.

To appreciate these lyrics, you should know that at several times each week in the summer, a ranger leads a nature walk into Annie Creek Canyon, a moderately deep ravine adjacent to the Mazama campground. At the bottom of the canyon is a small stream just a few feet wide flowing from a cold spring. The canyon trail follows the stream for about one half mile.

The amusement in the song is that the trail out of the canyon is strenuous, the stream is much too cold and small to swim, and except for minnow-size fish, they are nowhere about . . . Still, the rangers love to lead campers in singing the song and then the next day hike with the same campers into the canyon for a first-hand experience and more fun.

I never knew who wrote the lyrics or how old they were, but it goes like this:

Way down in Annie Creek Canyon
Way down in Annie Creek Canyon
You can hike, You can hike
All the trails are downhill
All the trails are downhill
Ho! Ho! Ho!, Ho! Ho! Ho!

Way down in Annie Creek Canyon
Way down in Annie Creek Canyon
You can fish, You can fish
All the fish are big ones
All the fish are big ones
Ho! Ho! Ho!, Ho! Ho! Ho!

Way down in Annie Creek Canyon
Way down in Annie Creek Canyon
You can swim, You can swim
The rangers heat the water
The rangers heat the water
Ho! Ho! Ho!, Ho! Ho! Ho!

Way down in Annie Creek Canyon
Way down in Annie Creek Canyon
You can hunt, You can hunt
Hunt jack-a-lopes and fire-bats
Hunt jack-a-lopes and fire-bats
Ho! Ho! Ho!, Ho! Ho! Ho!*

*The last part courtesy of the author, who has never even been to Crater Lake!

****

Oregon and Washington were formerly covered with little more than temperate rainforests and volcanoes except for their eastern halves, where lava-based grasslands stretch into Idaho. I could have included the *Gem of the Mountains* (Idaho) under the Rocky Mountains. Based on some of the visitors' questions I received from Idaho's Craters of the Moon National Monument, I might have grouped Idaho with the moon under Extraterrestrial Wilderness Areas.

Since the National Park Service doesn't yet manage any lunar-based wilderness areas, I chose to follow a third popular convention in classifying the *Land of Famous Potatoes* as a Pacific Northwest state. And since **Hagerman Fossil Beds National Monument** is in Idaho, this is where you can read about it.

No state honors horses as does Idaho. The Appaloosa is the official state horse. Contrary to popular belief, there is no evidence to indicate a particular association between the Appaloosa and Nez Perce Indians; it's simply a romantic fantasy created by white people.

Wizard Island does not float, though a portion of it does project above the surface of Crater Lake. The island is completely encircled by the lake, which is in turn encircled by a volcanic crater. Because the crater is concave, rather than convex, Crater Lake cannot be seen from the base of the mountain, which is covered with plants bearing green leaves.

The Appaloosa does boast Northwest connections however. The name Appaloosa derives from the Palouse Grasslands of eastern Washington and adjacent Idaho. There's even a Palouse River and, in Washington, a community called Palouse.

Another river with an equine connection is the Snake. Located along the banks of the Snake River, Hagerman Fossil Beds are world renowned for their abundant fossils of an animal variously described as a horse, zebra, or horse-zebra. It was adopted as Idaho's official fossil under the name "Hagerman Horse." This animal roamed the savannas of Idaho during the Pliocene Epoch, some three and a half million years ago. A ranger sent the following item.

> Hagerman Fossil Beds National Monument in south-central Idaho has a temporary visitor center with an interactive display for children. It is an elevated sand box in which we keep buried "fossil" bones so they can dig around and experience the excitement of a "find." This site is famous for the Hagerman Horse, the official state fossil.

> One day, a young boy was methodically locating every bone buried in the box and laying them out. He noticed there were five horse hooves and he looked up with an incredulous look and said, "Did these all come from the same horse?"

> Educationally, the most common misperception involves "change" in the environment. People have a tendency to think things have pretty much remained the same as they look today. We try to convey concepts like shifting continents over a molten earth, and our local volcanic activity is clearly visible. The layers of the Monument show remnants of one ancient flood after another about 3 million years ago, so we try to have them imagine this area when it was wetter, flatter, and there were many floods. It is now a high, Great Basin desert. The present landscape was formed only 15,000 years ago when the Bonneville Flood roared across the Snake River Plain, and exposed the fossils buried in the ancient floods. It takes a good imagination to envision the past.

It takes an even greater imagination to envision a chunk of the moon crashing into Earth and being designated a national park. Yet some visitors to Idaho's **Craters of the Moon National Monument** envision just that.

In fact, the Monument's features are evidence of volcanic activity, not lunar. The numerous questions and quips that follow are gleaned from the "I Can't Believe They Said That" book which staff have compiled over the years. Some items apparently assume a familiarity with the area, others with the moon.

Origins

When did this drop here from the moon?

What is Craters of the Moon?

"So did you take a plow through that?"
Through what, I asked.
"Through that black stuff that's all turned up." referring to the Aa flows.*

Had a guy come up to the desk rather disappointed and upset that they had drove 80 miles to see this place and all it was was lava. He wanted to see the crater in the earth that was made from a meteor.

Did lava come out of the ground? My husband said it came out of the air.

Is it hypothesis or fact that God's flood in Noah's time came from underneath the Earth's crust? I heard the crust is floating on a layer of water.

Did someone carve those faces on Mt. Rushmore?

Do you have any postcards of the nuclear blast over at that I.N.E.L. place?

Geology

Why are the rocks black?

Were these rocks placed here or have they always been here?

"Is that white stuff on the mountains volcanic ash?"
No, I replied, it's snow.
"Oh no," she replied, "I know volcanic ash when I see it."

What's the charcoal for? Is that to show that that's what this place is?
Do you have a rock sample for me or should I just help myself outside?

What's the difference between a geyser and a volcano?

*Aa is a type of lava.

"I've operated on kidney stones for 15 years, seen 'em magnified 30x, and this place is just like kidney stones. They're just minerals, too. Clear, but beautiful! You know Bing Crosby? He had a beautiful kidney stone. I saw it, just beautiful."

Flora & Fauna

Visitor informed me that the park had been shut down 2 years ago because of a rattlesnake infestation.

Can I talk to someone about rodents in my car?

Where is the nearest old-growth forest?

Getting About

A 13-mile round trip! From which end?

"How far off the road is 'Boy Scout Camp'?"
Answered ½ mile
"So the water is boiling in there?"

Those guys who hiked the Great Rift, how did they plant water? Did they dig holes with a shovel or what?
(These hikers cached plastic water containers along the trail.)

Now is that 7 mi Loop by vehicle or 7 mi by walking?
I saw a picture of a lake. Can you show me on the park map where it is?

Visitor told me we should warn people about the 10% grade — He had to drive back on the one-way road because of his fear of heights. Said we should do something about it! (Perhaps, we could eliminate it when we do the new road!)

I'm sure the Curey-Kimama or Arco-Minidoka road would be the faster way to get south to Utah.

Would it be OK to land an airplane out here on the road and pull it into your parking lot? (Serious question)

Scott & I are watching a movie at 9:30 pm in the lunch room when some guy drives up, pokes his head in the door & says, "Is this the campground?"

Harnessing Nature's Forces

Is it true that the Navy tests its submarines in the aquifer under the Snake River Plains?

Is it the lava that powers that energy place (the INEL) by Idaho Falls?

Tourist Tip: At Craters of the Moon National Monument, submarines always have the right of way — unless you're driving a moon rover.

Tourists Will Be Tourists

Found a video camera today. We played the tape & saw Dad collecting rocks right in front of a do-not-collect-rocks sign. They came in to see if we had found the camera. Heh Heh Heh. Sure! We'll give you the camera if you give us the rocks. Mom says, "We didn't take rocks! Only pebbles!" Dad says, "I thought the sign meant 'Don't take rocks <u>Behind</u> the sign,' I thought the rocks from in <u>front</u> of the sign were okay." All we wanted was for them to admit what they did was wrong. We almost cited them, but we finally let them go (We gave them the camera back, too). We're so nice...

Park personnel are baffled by the mysterious appearance of a vehicle axle in the restroom lobby during the morning shift. Chief Ranger Bruce Edmonston makes positive I.D. of unit. Axle was picked up in afternoon — 2 parties meeting halfway to get a vehicle repaired, figured this was logical place to cache it. No note to us, though.

My theory on why all of the Visitor's seem so weird today — is that the smoke is so heavy in the air — they are all breathing too deep & getting high

IE: One man wanted to go in the Indian Tunnel then started to sweat as I was telling him about it, then said he had claustrophobia.
IE: One annoying woman wanted me to choose which hat she should get her male friend.
IE: A nearly deaf man took his hearing help dog on the trail with him & a woman got mad at him for it.

Philosophy

(Visitors seated in front lobby with dog) We thought this wasn't really <u>inside</u> the building.

Why do people camp here?

Freebies?

Are these books for sale?

Where are the books for sale? (standing right by book racks)

A gentleman standing at the V.C. counter: Is there a place here where you sell books?

You know what? I was going to take one of those. (Looking at KC's) I thought they were really nice brochures!

Do I pay you for these books or just put it in the [Donation] box there?

Are these national parks books (KC) for sale or giveaways?

Can I have a plan?

Does it get dark here?

Can I please have a Golden Egg?
(French visitor — Kiosk)

Missileaneous

"Can you camp here?" Yes "Overnight?"

(Visitor with water jug, gesturing toward lobby) Is the water drinkable here?

Oh, where do you ski?" (woman after noticing my SCA patch)

That sign out there on the scenic overlook says nothing about the flow or anything anyone's interested in — it just talks about air pollution.

(Teenage daughter, looking at ozone monitor): What's this?
Father: A weather station.
Daughter: Is this for life on the moon or what?

When will you be able to become financially independent here at the park, from the government and Dept. of Interior? (Author's note: See possible answer below.)

"Can I have a copy of your hunting regulations?"
You can't hunt here.
"I know, but can I have a copy of your regulations?"
The regulation is: You can't hunt here.
"But can I have a copy of the regulations?"*

*Why don't Craters of the Moon's staff make a "HUNTING REGULATIONS" brochure that folds out to reveal the words "NO HUNTING ALLOWED" and sell it for 25 cents? Such a brochure could be sold in all the national parks. It could take a chunk out of our national debt.

CRATERS of the MOON
Tri-Annual Guided Missile Lunar
Jack-a-lope Non-Hunting Season

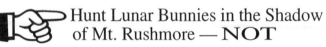 Hunt Lunar Bunnies in the Shadow of Mt. Rushmore — **NOT**

Inquire about our registered lava non-guides
(Why not? They've been inquiring about you!)

SPECIAL SURPRISE TOPIC:
Spotlight on Pacific Northwest Symbols

That Washingtonians are proud of their state's natural and cultural diversity is evidenced by their state symbols. Take the state's name and flag — please — or the nonexistent state animal.

Washington State was named by an eastern politician. The state motto alludes to New York. The state bird, the goldfinch, also represents Iowa and New Jersey. Oregonians suggested Washington's state tree after they preempted that mainstay of the timber economy, the Douglas fir, which today graces Oregonian license plates.

Unfortunately, no one has ever given Washington a state animal. Inspired by North Dakota's northern pike, desperate Washingtonians decided they would adopt one all by themselves.

In 1982 legislator Paul Sanders, backed by hunters, the Department of Game, and the Elks Lodge, introduced legislation to name the Roosevelt elk the state animal.* Sanders was inspired to politically empower the quarry he had hunted when he was younger after another legislator tried, unsuccessfully, to enthrone the sea otter as the Evergreen State's mammal-in-chief the previous year.

The spectacular Roosevelt elk, a subspecies, is unique to Washington. With such qualifications, the elk bill passed the House 65-27. A stuffed elk brought by Sanders for the occasion wasn't allowed on the House floor. (Thomas Jefferson once sent a stuffed moose to a European intellectual to counter the latter's claim that North America's fauna is generally inferior to Old World fauna.)

Ironically, the elk's House victory carried with it the twin seeds of its destruction — politics and biodiversity. Democratic Representative Gene Lux moved to amend Sander's bill by striking the scientific name *Cervus elaphus roosevelti* and substituting "elfranco delaphos roosevelti." "Franklin Delano Roosevelt was a wonderful president of the United States," responded Sanders as cheers broke out on the Democratic side of the aisle. "But the Roosevelt elk was not named

*The Roosevelt elk is also known as the Olympic elk, not because it is particularly athletic but because it is at home on Washington's Olympic Peninsula.

for a Democratic president, it was named for a Republican president, Theodore Roosevelt."

Sanders also made a critical error when he nominated the Roosevelt elk for the office of state *animal*. Such a designation would be acceptable in almost any state but Washington, where mollusks are more prominent than mammals, which themselves may be politically allied with Eastern Washington, Western Washington, Seattle's Woodland Park Zoo, or Puget Sound. In the meantime, the scent of politics in the air brought the press to a feeding frenzy.

On the day before Groundhog Day, *Seattle Post Intelligencer* ("P-I") columnist Jon Hahn wrote, "The bipartisan bicameral bipeds have once again completed their cyclical migration to Olympia, where they will spawn new generations of mutant taxes, regulations, policies, bureaucracies and idiocies, not the least of which is a renewed effort to have some insurance company's animal emblem named the Washington State Animal." Hahn favored the mountain beaver.

Lewis and Clark coined "sewellel" in 1806 as a corruption of a Chinook word that actually describes a robe made of the animal skins, rather than a living animal. Yet that name is more accurate than *mountain beaver*, for this strange creature is neither. Whether you call it a mountain beaver, an aplodontia, or a robe, it is an enigma.

The sole member of the family Aplodontidae, the mountain beaver may be the world's most primitive rodent. It also boasts the largest known fleas, named for a Washingtonian, Theo H. Scheffer.

Not the least intimidated by huge fleas, staffers in the state House Republican communications office launched an informal campaign for the Lincoln mole. *Mole Movement* members organized a mole joke contest to promote the mole and spoof the elk.

Q. How can you pick out the mole in a herd of elk?
A. He's the one with the false antlers.

Moles were also advertised as "handier" than elk. "Moles can be given to visitors and sent to relatives in other states," noted Rudolph. "Can you imagine what it costs to ship an elk to Kansas?"

A few years ago, students from Seattle's Cleveland High School, under the misguidance of a school board member, tried to promote a giant ground sloth named for Thomas Jefferson as state fossil. Fortunately, legislators had the wisdom to pass up their generous offer. On second thought, such a designation wouldn't have been totally stupid.

With its Roosevelt elk, Lincoln mole, and Jefferson ground sloth, Washington deserves its own Mt. Rushmore. Washingtonians ought to carve a Cascade peak into a flag, elk, mole, and sloth. Students could match the icon with the president, combining geology, natural history, social studies, and art (see picture on page 7).

Most state animals are mammals, but Washington is not most states. The elk's biggest competitor turned out to be a giant clam known as the geoduck. This enormous, long-lived gastropod was declared by the *Seattle Post-Intelligencer* as Washington's *real* "clam-to-fame."

The geoduck-elk confrontation was advertised as "bipartisan bivalve vs mammal with a politically identifiable past." The specter of the mighty Olympic elk being challenged by a bivalve must have made IVAR's beam with pride.*

Writing in the *Seattle Times* (February 28, 1982), Lee Larrick endorsed the slug, long an unofficial symbol of the *Emerald City*, Seattle.

I also believe that a day should be set aside honoring the animal of our choice. We could do it early in February and call it "Ground Slug's Day." Possibly future generations will build up a fiction related to the noble animal — something about seeing its shadow, thereby prolonging our wet season on into June or July or August.

Another slug afficionado suggested that a slug be depicted on Washington's already sluggish flag — "A mauve slug on our state flag? It's so-o-o-o modern."

The Pacific Northwest is the slug capital of the world. (Snails love the high rainfall, but have a hard time growing shells due to the calcium-poor soil. Thus, they evolved into slugs, as do many Washingtonians in winter.)

*IVAR's is a local seafood restaurant chain whose namesake, the late Ivar Haglund, was known for his sense of humor. "Keep clam" is IVAR's motto.

Washingtonians might embrace an official slug as a deterrent to immigrants, similar to Alaska's unofficial state bird, the mosquito. Let's add Seattle Representative Jeff Douthwaite's proposed official weather forecast — 90% chance of rain — and devil's club, the Pacific Northwest's most formidable shrub — even the roots have spines!

As unpredictable as sunshine, Washingtonians might astound the world by enthroning a state animal with a backbone after all. The *Seattle P-I* printed readers' suggestions. The turkey, pig, and buzzard were suggested because they reminded readers of legislators. One reader noted that Washington already has a state seal. "I vote for the bear, because its reaction to people moving into its territory is the same as mine," wrote one territorial reader. The expanding development of nuclear plants, Boeing aircraft, and the Trident submarine base prompted another reader to suggest the "Sitting Duck." The P-I printed a picture of a composite "Washington Whatsis" with body parts from a moose, beaver, and duck.

Few of the candidates in Washington's great state animal debate of 1982 were representative of Eastern Washington, a Pacific Northwest version of Dakota Territory. Nor is yet another candidate — Sasquatch, or Bigfoot. This relative of the Himalayan *yeti* or "abominable snowman" served as Washington's official Centennial mascot.

But Washington already has an official mammal. The state is named for him. Which reminds me of Washington's state flag, which brings us back to rain and slugs. Do Washingtonians cling to their God-awful flag because it complements rain and slugs in discouraging immigrants from settling in their *Ecotopia*?

Deep inside, most Washingtonians agree with me. Wave a Texas State flag at Mount Rainier National Park and watch Texan visitors snap to attention. Wave a Washington State flag at the Alamo and watch Washingtonians pretend they don't see it.

Another garish state flag many residents wish would go away is Idaho's. Perhaps the most complex of all state flags, it is said to be flown — along with neighboring Montana's flag — less frequently than any other state flag due to the resulting expense of manufacture.

Spokesman-Review (Spokane, Washington) columnist Paul Turner says many of his readers — both Washingtonians and Idahoans — complain about their flags. In the February 19, 1994 issue, he presented whimsical designs created by local sixth-graders, "to replace Washington's boring state flag." Ironically, one design that lacked George is arguably more attractive than the present flag and would be cheaper to manufature to boot. "Now if we can just get somebody to work on Idaho's flag," Turner commented.

(Above) The author's proposed Washington State flag relieves the green background with a blue stripe between two yellow stripes to represent the sea and the grasslands of Eastern Washington. A distinctive Pacific Northwest icon, the totem pole suggests living things and cultural diversity. It spans the design's elements, reminding us of Chief Sealth's (Seattle's namesake) words, "All things are connected." The totem pole's form and color are problematic. Gary Csillaghegyi suggests it be modeled after a totem pole on the capitol grounds in Olympia. Or it could be left blank, allowing viewers to imbue it with whatever meaning they choose. It is generally not considered proper to place symbols on a flag's fly, the side that flaps freely in the wind. The star's irrational placement therefore suggests individuality and that elusive thing called freedom, along with snow-capped mountains

Neither Washington nor Idaho has a state animal. Neither Washington nor Idaho *needs* a state animal. But can someone from the East, the Dakotas, Alaska — anywhere — donate a suitable flag to either state? Such flags ought to be reasonably simple, distinctive, symbolically appropriate, and attractive. They should especially celebrate the wilderness and diversity for which the Pacific Northwest is so justly renowned. They should be flags that Park Rangers would be proud to show — maybe even sell — to visitors.

(Above) The elk on the author's proposed Idaho state flag is taken from the state seal. Chevrons suggest the *Gem of the Mountains'* rugged topography. They are colored, from top to bottom, blue, yellow, green to represent waters, grasslands, and forests. Snow-capped mountains are suggested by the white background, along with the star, which further suggests the nickname *Gem of the Mountains*. The star also commemorates the state flower and gem, Syringa and star garnet.

ALASKA
Where Men Are Men

I heard a story about an Alaska governor who, angry at a Texas governor, threatened to divide Alaska in half, making Texas the third biggest state. With its enormous size and small population, Alaska fits in nicely with one of this book's minor themes, wilderness. More importantly, Alaska boasts one of the most beautiful state flags. Alaska even competes with the civilized East as a center of culture: The last battle of the Civil War was fought in Alaska. Unfortunately, no monument marks the site of the battle, which occurred at sea.*

This book was originally planned as a three-volume set, one volume covering forty-nine states, the other two Alaska. Unfortunately, only one Alaskan responded to my request for humorous material.

Having worked in Alaska, I have a few personal experiences to relate. However, I decided to save this material for a sequel. Hopefully, it will be complemented with material provided by some of the rangers, cannery workers, bird dog owners, fishermen, trappers, dogmushers, bush pilots, wildlife biologists, avalanche dynamics experts, hockey players, snowmobile dealers, pipeline technicians, and oil spill cleanup experts who call America's Last Frontier home — for at least three months out of the year.

Until the sequel is published, all the glory for contributing irrational material from our wildest — and therefore most rational — state goes to one anonymous correspondent.

Let me introduce this contribution by saying that I spent two summers in the nation's largest wildlife refuge — including watery expanses between islands — the **Alaska Maritime National Wildlife Refuge**. The first summer I worked in the Semidis, a small group of islands west of Kodiak Island, which was and is a great seabird colony noted especially for its puffins. It was there that I learned the truth about those spectacular beaks. They're fake! Like false fingernails, puffins shed these gaudy displays after the mating season to reveal ordinary bird beaks.

---

*Readers who believe, as I do, that the federal government should establish a monument to this battle are invited to submit suggestions for the name and nature of such a monument. Address correspondence to: Alaska Civil War Monument, Geobopological Survey, PO Box 95465, Seattle, WA 98145.

Frequently perceived as somewhat comical, puffins are a popular motif in Alaskan pop art. "No Puffin" signs can be purchased in stores in lieu of "No Smoking" signs, for example. An employee of the U.S. Fish and Wildlife Service contributes the following items.

While standing on deck of boats on Kachemak Bay tourists often ask "What elevation are we at?" The best response I have found is to deliberately look over the edge and answer "Oh, about 10 feet above sea level!" Sometimes they get it, sometimes they don't.

Many helpful souls rescue "abandoned" seal pups and proudly bring them to the Visitor Center. It is always hard to explain that their helpfulness may cost the seal its life as mothers leave their young on beaches while they fish and expect them to still be there when they return. Human scent often discourages mother seals from accepting their young.

My favorite [remark] comes from a couple who entered the VC [visitor center] and spied a mounted tufted puffin on the desk. The woman exclaimed "Oh honey look! A TOUCAN!" Her husband confidently replied "That's not a toucan, that's a MUFFIN!"

. . . Visitors who drive to Homer follow the Sterling Highway. This road overlooks the Cook Inlet and has spectacular views of the Chigmit Mountains, a range that connects the Alaska Range (Denali) with the Alaska Peninsula Range. I don't know what road map one individual looked at but when he [finally] arrived . . ., he excitedly asked "Was that Russia we saw on the way down here?"

We (along with everyone else, I assume) constantly are asked "Where do you keep the animals?" When I was working at **Kenai** NWR [**National Wildlife Refuge**] one couple was especially persistent. They finally asked if I had a moose tied up in back. I tried to explain the difference between a wildlife refuge and a petting zoo. I don't know if it worked.

One I just heard about came from the Fairbanks Public Lands Information Center. A visitor was asking questions about visiting the musk ox farm and asked "Will I be able to see woolly mammoths there?"

HAWAII
Back to Arizona?

If the entire state of Hawaii were designated a national park, it could still scarcely be considered wilderness, for how can one get lost on Maui, Oahu, or even the Big Island? Yet the Hawaiian Islands encompass some of the National Park Service's hottest assets. More than mere curiosities, these active volcanoes are a wise investment: over time, they will continue to enlarge the National Park Service's far-flung empire as they ooze hot lava — "liquid real estate." Hopefully, present or former guardians of Hawaii's volcanoes will enlarge my collection of volcano humor, which includes nothing from Hawaii — even though I once climbed to the top of Mauna Loa and was promptly gripped with altitude sickness.

Hawaii is our most exotic state. Surfing, hula dancing, pineapples, active volcanoes that enlarge national parks — they're all a part of Hawaii, as are the numerous introduced species that are driving native Hawaiian species to extinction.

It's hard to believe such a fantasy land could ever have known the taste of war. Yet Pearl Harbor represents the greatest assault on American soil in recent history. On December 7, 1941 Japanese planes launched a surprise attack on Pearl Harbor, where almost the entire Pacific fleet was moored. They sank or severely damaged nineteen vessels, destroyed numerous airplanes, and killed more than 2,400 military personnel and 49 civilians. The attack goaded the United States into World War II.

The only ship permanently lost was the 26-year-old battleship USS *Arizona*. Its watery grave is marked by a floating memorial, owned by the U.S. Navy and administered by the National Park Service.

While visiting Hawaii, I heard the following story: A Japanese dignitary who was visiting Hawaii asked a marine guard, "Can you tell me please, where is the *Arizona*?" The marine snapped, "It's right where you left it!"

A contributor who is anonymous even to me sent a list of humorous questions asked at the Memorial. I've rearranged them. Aloha.

VISITOR QUESTIONS AND COMMENTS
AT THE USS ARIZONA MEMORIAL

First Things First

Is that the real Arizona?

Where is the Arizona now?

Is the Arizona inside the Memorial?

(Point to the Ford Island Ferry) Is that the Arizona?

Did they tow the Arizona over there?

Is the Memorial in the sun? If so, I don't want to go on the tour, I've had enough sun.

Where is the elevator to take you underwater to see the Arizona?

Can we walk out to the Arizona?

Why don't you move the Memorial closer to shore so that the visitors can walk to it?

Why did they build the Memorial way out in the water?

Did they build the Memorial before or after the ship sank?

What is the name of the ship under the Arizona Memorial?

What does the state of Arizona have to do with the attack on Pearl Harbor?

What was named first, the state or the battleship?

The Arizona's Contents

Are there men entombed in the walls of the Memorial?

Are the dead men on the ship buried in coffins?

Are there still people alive on the Arizona?

When did the Arizona's bell float up?

Do bones still float up?

Does the oil keep the ship from rusting?

Do you add oil to the ship to keep it leaking?

Is it true that when the oil stops leaking WWIII will start?

Is it true that you can't smoke on the Memorial because of the leaking oil?

On Tour

Do the tour numbers go in sequence?

What does, "first come, first served" mean?

What if they call my tour number while I'm in the movie?

Are you sure that the tour is free?

I don't want to go on the tour, I just want to see the movie and the Memorial.

How will you know my name when its time to call me for the tour?

How will they know where to find us when they call our number over the P.A.?

What time does the 9:45 tour leave?

How come you told me the tour takes an hour and 15 minutes and the other ranger said that it only takes 75 minutes?

Miscellaneous

What do you see in the theater?

Do they show the movie in the theater?

Is Ford Island completely surrounded by water?

Do you speak and understand English?

After the shuttle boat leaves me on the Memorial, how do I get back?

Extra Attractions

Where is the Memorial to Semper Fidelis, the first man to fight?

Where do you people do weddings?

Where do the submarine rides leave from?

Do your tour boats go to Waikiki Beach?

Where is the Arizona Memorial Restaurant where the Elvis Presley impersonator is performing?

Do you have a dolphin show here?

(Upset visitor on the Memorial) Aren't we supposed to get a cruise on the Arizona?

(Visitor with coupon from Waikiki Beach) Where is my free hot dog?

(Irate visitor) Do we get a free meal served on the tour?

Can we take the Arizona to the Pearl Ridge Shopping Center?

The End

"Where do I go when I'm all through?"

Pearl Harbor: 'When is the dolphin show?'
By Jack Schnedler, Travel Editor
Chicago Sun-Times, September 8, 1991
Reprinted with permission, *Chicago Sun-Times* © 1995

While researching his new book, *Pearl Harbor Ghosts*, Thurston Clarke discovered that National Park Service rangers at the USS Arizona Memorial keep a secret "blooper book."* It records some of the astonishing questions asked by American tourists who visit the sunken battleship, which exploded with the loss of 1,177 U.S. lives in the Japanese attack on Dec. 7, 1941:"

"I'm a bit confused. I thought I was in Hawaii...then what's all this Arizona business?"

"Can you tell me how often the bodies float up?"

"So this is a Japanese ship that we sunk, huh?"

"Hi! I want to see if the Arizona is in port today."

"Why didn't they tow the Arizona to Waikiki? It'd be much more convenient to visit it there."

"What time is the dolphin show?"

Clarke finds such apogees of American ignorance both laughable and appalling — especially so at a national memorial that is also a cemetery for the remains of 1,102 crewmen whose bodies were never recovered. Writing as Pearl Harbor braces for a surge of tourists during 50th-anniversary commemorations three months from now, he approaches the matter by way of the half-million Japanese who visit the Arizona each year.

If anything, judges Clarke, "the Japanese behaved better at the Arizona than most nationalities do when visiting sightseeing attractions in large groups. But the problem was the nature of the attraction. Because they had come to the grave of men killed by a Japanese generation still alive, actions that at Disneyland or the Grand Canyon would seem harmless, or even commendable, became irritating or sinister."

*Author's note: My anonymous correspondent advises me, "Book long since lost!"

His book cites a number of these "annoying" Japanese actions:

•Their tendency to march behind a guide carrying a flag, which "struck me as unnecessarily martial."
•Their "perverse" fondness for buying plastic models of the Arizona at the gift shop.
•Their custom "of pitching small-denomination Japanese coins onto the Arizona's submerged decks."
•Their habit "of gathering around the scale model in a tight knot — so tight there was no room for me — while their guide pointed with a flagpole to where the bomb had struck. They paid too much attention to this lengthy briefing. There were too many murmurs of agreement and nodding of heads, an interest unseemly in its intensity, and one feeding my suspicion some had come to celebrate a victory."

But Clarke's perspective shifts as he watches Americans visiting the Arizona:

"While most Japanese wore sober suits, modest skirts or polo shirts, Americans came in tank tops, tube socks and sweatshirts, in cutoff blue jeans, jogging shorts and bathing shorts. They wore plastic visors that turned their faces green, and novelty T-shirts with four-letter words. I watched them pick up tickets for the shuttle boat, and saw looks of amazement and disgust on those turned away for failing to meet the minimal requirement of 'shirts, shorts and footwear.'"

The more Clarke compares the Japanese to the American visitors, "the better the Japanese looked and the more obvious it became that if anyone was desecrating this place, it was us." He observes that "the people asking the ignorant questions about 'dolphin shows' that found their way into the rangers' 'blooper book' were Americans."

Some of the problem, he suggests, may lie with the tone set by the joint National Park Service-U.S. Navy operation at the Pearl Harbor location:

"The shuttle boats taking visitors out to the memorial were piloted by American sailors who described the sinking of the Arizona in the bored monotone of a flight attendant, adding as they docked, 'Have a nice day.' (Ask yourself, if you were leaving a group at the cemetery, would you tell them to have a 'nice day'?)"

The Pearl Harbor Ghosts author also points to the memorial's design — an open white bridge spanning the wreckage — as "somewhat to blame for the lack of respect shown by some American visitors. It is a striking structure, even a beautiful one, but it lacks the necessary morbidity, the power to move even the most ignorant to tears."

Perhaps, says Clarke, U.S. authorities at the Arizona Memorial should post "the kind of austere signs the French have erected at Verdun: 'You Are Entering the Actual Battlefield. This Earth Has Been Drenched with the Blood of Thousands of Heroes. They Demand the Homage of Your Silence.'"

In the face of such a message, he doubts that "this place would have become a wishing well" for coin-tossing Japanese and American visitors, "or just another stop on the Honolulu tourist agenda."

(Japanese tour guide) "The Memorial was built across the ship to hold it down and keep it from floating away."

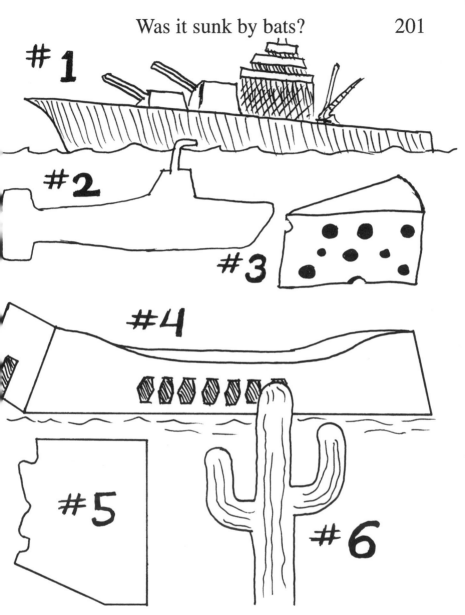

The USS *Arizona* is a ship, similar to #1, except that it is underwater, similar to a submarine (#2) and is full of holes, similar to cheese (#3). The USS *Arizona* Memorial is a Memorial, similar to #4. And #5 is an outline of the state of Arizona. If you're still confused, just look around. If you see a saguaro cactus (#6) you are in the state of Arizona.

Congratulations! You've reached the end — or have you? Like Robert Frost, you've come to a fork in the road. Which path will you choose? Decide carefully; your choice may indicate something about your personality. Although only you can make this choice, Robert Frost's poem *The Road Not Taken* offers some valuable advice.

ENDING #1
Black Bear (*Ursus americanus*)

ENDING #2
Grizzly Bear (*Ursus horribilis*)

BEYOND THE END

Did you really think this book would end? Ends are for dead-end roads and political terms. Garbage dumps are ends. So are prisons, drug abuse, and efforts to halt Congressional corruption. This book is about Nature and Nature is all about cycles, which contrary to popular belief are best represented by spirals rather than circles, and recycling.

But more than Nature, this book is also about American civilization and where it's heading. Our national parks and public schools are guardians of two of civilization's most vital components, wilderness and literacy, which continue to erode under an onslaught of political and bureaucratic neglect and outright stupidity. It's time for Americans to stand up on their hind legs and do something.

Curing a problem begins with two things: 1) Recognizing the problem, and 2) making choices. This book is but an introduction to the greatest crisis threatening life on Earth since whatever it was that wiped out the dinosaurs.

By exercising your rights as a United States citizen in selecting the ending of your choice, you acted in the tradition of the colonists who told King George to stick it, those who defended the Alamo against overwhelming odds, and the rangers and teachers who daily fight the insidious enemies of civilization that threaten the Republic as no foreign power ever did.

The ending you chose may indicate something about your personality, your constitution, even your fitness to survive. In short, offering two endings was a test. Read the sequel to learn how you scored.

AFTERWORD

Writing this book has changed my attitude towards tourists. Of course, no one likes a truly rude, obnoxious visitor, nor does anyone want to deal with tourists in overwhelming numbers (except Wall Drug employees, who take on as many as 20,000 paying customers a day).

Perhaps as offensive as the rudest visitors is the person who has been everywhere, done everything, and knows all there is to know. "Yea, I climbed in the Himalayas." (Yawn.) "Yea, I kayaked in Glacier Bay; my father owns a guide company there." (Yawn.) "I studied mountain gorillas before embarking on a geological survey of the Northwest Territories." This person's eyes remain jaded at the spectacle of an animal giving birth ("seen it before"), the sound of an elk bugling in Wyoming ("used to live there"), or the scent of a delicate blossom. "I have nothing left to live for."

But you know what? Rude, obnoxious tourists and people who are all *touristed out* and are yearning for a new life (how about on a different planet?) amount to a tiny minority of humanity. Most tourists are decent people doing what all normal people have a yen to do — seeing and experiencing a planet that cannot be fully seen and experienced in a million lifetimes. Veteran rangers, guides, wildlife biologists, geologists, spelunkers, and anyone who visits a place they've never seen before or dares to experience a new experience becomes a tourist. Put Sir Edmund Hillary, conqueror of Mt. Everest, or the astronauts who visited the moon in Everglades National Park and they would be transformed into ordinary tourists.

Employees of the National Park Service and allied agencies are charged with several missions. They must, of course, protect the wilderness and its inhabitants, and they must regulate the vast numbers of tourists who visit these places annually.

But a ranger's highest calling is environmental education. The job greatly exceeds merely reciting facts and figures, entreating to conserve and protect, and disseminating faunal, botanical, geological, and historical trivia. A ranger, you see, has the rare opportunity to be a magician, the portal to the supernatural lying through "the eyes."

"The eyes" are manifested more frequently on some individuals than others — virtually no adult is permanently endowed with them. "The eyes" typically disappear for great periods of time during middle-age, when people are engrossed with the day-to-day demands of work and raising a family, but reappear in life's twilight.

They are the eyes of a child reborn, someone who has, even if just for a minute, regained the capacity to look at the world with a sense of curiosity and a capacity for awe. They are the eyes that transform a playground into a magical kingdom more wondrous than any national park. They are the eyes that make us forget about bills and traffic jams and all the jerks and bureaucracies that have screwed up our lives — even the IRS, which relieves us of our hard-earned money so that the government, in all its stupidity and wretchedness, can throw it away (as if taxpayers couldn't do that themselves).

They are the eyes that ask questions most grown-ups would be embarrassed to ask under ordinary circumstances: "What would it be like to ride an avalanche or a pterosaur?" "How long could I survive in this wilderness without store-bought food or clothing?" "What would it be like to swim like an otter and catch fish with my teeth?"

For several years, I've worked as a teacher in an urban school district wallowing in bureaucracy and tyrannized by administrators who prove time and again that they really don't care about the children they're charged with caring for and care even less for the teachers, parents, and select administrators who comprise the only segment of the organization that functions. I suspect there are many school districts across the nation *parasitized* by similar administrations. (I've often wished our administrators would pack their bags and go on an extended tour of our national parks, letting us teachers get on with our work. Observing rangers might teach them something about interpersonal relations.)*

There *is* one thing I like about this school district: the children. They possess the eyes. Children are permanent residents of a world of

---

*There are certainly numerous administrators who are decent human beings. My tirade is aimed against the central bureaucracy, a handful of principals, and those rare teachers who have been brainwashed into believing that administrators should not be held accountable for their actions. Let's blame all of America's problems on teachers and environmentalists!

make-believe and magic and, in their company, so am I. They awaken me to a force that animates even the inanimate.

I sometimes fantasize about taking a group of children on a field-trip to Alaska or the Great Barrier Reef, maybe even Madagascar. As much as I'd like to see a herd of caribou in migration — a spectacle I missed when I worked in Alaska — a Madagascan lemur, or a sea-horse, I would enjoy the spectacle so much more if I could see it through the eyes of children.

I may never be able to afford to jet off to Madagascar with a plane-load of children. But I can explore the universe without leaving my classroom. The next best thing is to work in a national park, greeting carloads of tourists, adults and children alike. Sure, some of them may be grouchy after a long day's drive. That's only natural. Sure, many of them may be ignorant. God bless them! Ignorance only increases the likelihood that they will have the eyes...

Imagine stepping into *The Twilight Zone*. It's one minute to open-ing. You are a ranger confronted with a line of cars stretching to the horizon. You brace yourself for the usual requests for directions, times, and fees, punctuated here and there by a remarkable question about Nature's wonders.

The first person you greet looks neither tired nor excited; his coun-tenance suggests boredom. With jaded eyes he says, "I really don't care to see the crater. I've seen craters before." He yawns and drives on. The next visitor unexcitedly informs you, "I know more about this park's wildlife than you do, ranger; I wrote a book about it."

For five hours you greet jaded visitors who would not be out of place on an industrial assembly line. The look on everyone's face seems to say, "Are you as bored with your job as I am with my life?"

You feel useless, despised, impotent. Your miserly wage suddenly *seems* miserly. "You made the wrong career choice!" your brain screams as you begin reassessing your life goals. Here you are in one of America's most spectacular oases and you're feeling as jaded as the visitors! You close your eyes in despair. "What's going on? Where am I?"

"Hey ranger, was this here crater made by a meteor or a nuclear blast? Or was it a meteor that produced a nuclear blast? Is the center of the crater in the middle? And how about the animals — are they radioactive?"

In disbelief, you look up to see someone with *the eyes*. In the back seat are two children, their eyes eagerly anticipating your answer. You smile, your self-respect intact, as you prepare to work your magic.

APPENDIX

Endangered Rangers?

Americans have grown accustomed to uniformed rangers greeting, advising, educating, entertaining, guiding, and protecting them at our national parks, monuments, seashores, lakeshores, historic sites, and forests. In fact, many Americans take rangers for granted.

When you plan your next vacation, you might want to pack gifts for the National Park Service and USDA Forest Service employees that cater to you. Farewell gifts.

"Are rangers a thing of the past?" you ask incredulously. Of course not. Our legally sanctioned wilderness areas couldn't survive without rangers. And without national parks, monuments, forests, and wildlife refuges, American civilization couldn't survive.

Even so, these outposts of civilization continue to wither under assault by the forces of bureaucracy, greed, stupidity, and the general pressures exerted by a nation whose human residents number over a quarter of a billion, a statistic that America's 18th-century bison herds and the Southwest's pre-Civil War free-tailed bats combined can't begin to compete with. The continuing decline of some of Americans' favorite animals in the very places where they should feel most at home is an ominous warning of things to come.

Most national parks, monuments, forests, and wildlife refuges already lack one or more native species and have for years. No visitor to a nature preserve east of the Missouri River will ever kneel in awe as an approaching storm cloud suddenly transforms into an incomprehensible mass of passenger pigeons. Rare is the national park, even in the West, where one can glimpse so much as a footprint of a grizzly bear or wolf.

But for better or worse, people are adaptable. No wolves? People simply forget wolves ever lived in the area. No passenger pigeons? "What's a passenger pigeon?" No otters? "Maybe they're just hibernating." (Otters don't hibernate.) As long as a wilderness preserve boasts mountains or flatlands, forests or grasslands, or nondescript wastelands where animals can be thought to be lying buried under sand or hiding in lava crevices, people will visit it. And let's face it — some people *prefer* their wilderness sanitized of wild animals.

No. National parks, monuments, forests, and wildlife refuges will not disappear simply because there are no wild animals to inhabit them, and people will continue to visit wilderness areas regardless of the authenticity of their ecosystems and the crowds they must share the wilderness with. And these visitors — along with the wilderness areas they visit — will always need rangers. My concern is not that rangers may disappear, but that they may evolve.

The realization hit me like a thunderclap while reading the April 3, 1995 issue of *U.S. News & World Report*. In all honesty, I've never been an avid reader of this magazine, not because it's not worthwhile but because I'm simply too busy. When I do read magazines, they're generally tabloids that reveal secrets of poison arrow frogs in the Amazon or the sex lives of nurse sharks, the sorts of things all American citizens should know if they want to live in harmony with our global environment.

On the rare occasions when I do read *U.S. News & World Report*, I react to the Business section the way a typical tourist would react to a particular patch of grassland alongside Interstate 90 in South Dakota. But while browsing through the above-mentioned issue, I just happened to notice — in the Business section — a photo of Yosemite National Park with some fabulous granite monolith (the infamous Half Dome, I presume) in the top center. If national parks and business seem an incongruous combination, the article's message was downright unsettling.

The authors explore the possibility of combatting the national budget deficit by privatizing certain government programs. At first thought, such an idea exhilarates me. Having been employed by various bureaucracies (including the U.S. Navy, whose monumental stupidity is rivaled only by some of the other bureaucracies for which I've worked) I like the idea of turning these bureaucracies over to private citizens, who will be free to jump-start these dawdling, tottering, bizarre and therefore humorous enterprises with a quality they've never known before — intelligence.

Can you imagine a National Park Service or USDA Forest Service run by people who actually discourage road-building within their preserves? Or a public school district whose administrators actually assist teachers, rather than sabotaging their efforts to educate America's youth? Seems too good to be true? Perhaps it is.

Let's face it, the nonmilitary, non-civil servant majority isn't always what it's cracked up to be. Sure, there are honest, law-abiding, hard-working people out there. But our society is also cursed with dishonest, lawless loafers. Such people plague all societies.

But the *Capitalist Republic* for which our flag stands breeds a quality that few, if any, other nations can match in grandeur: greed. Probably no other nation celebrates greed — along with its corollary, arrogance — as we Americans do. Do any personalities come to mind?

Privatizing our national parks and monuments would be like playing dice. If ownership or jurisdiction falls into the hands of people with integrity who understand and love the wilderness, then American civilization might experience a renaissance. Or we might wind up with a Yellowstone National Park Corporation with Donald Trump as President and Rush Limbaugh as Public Relations Czar and Certified Expert on Trees and Other Natural Resources. Think about that as you read the following excerpt.

Yellowstone Irrational Park, Inc.?

Reversing the Tide
Washington Turns to Privatization to help reduce the budget deficit

by David Hage, Warren Cohen, Robert F. Black
U.S. News & World Report, April 3, 1995
Excerpt reprinted with permission of *U.S. News & World Report*

"Market forces that work powerfully in housing may not work as well in the wilderness. Or so Roger Kennedy assumed when he presented the National Park Service's 1996 budget to Congress last month. Much to his surprise, the park service director was asked by committee Republicans to produce a price list that set a market value on each of the nation's 368 park units. 'But how,' wonders Kennedy, 'do you put a price tag on the Washington Monument?'*

"In fact, privatizing national parks doesn't make sense to most economists — and not just because Americans would balk at the idea of putting Old Faithful in private hands.** For one thing, taxpayers already get a good deal from having parks in the public domain. Half of the National Park Service's full-time rangers work for less than $22,000 a year, even though most have specialized college degrees and put in long hours. Genial rangers in the familiar park service uniforms 'are one of the best bureaucracies around,' declares Harvard University political scientist John Donahue, precisely because they view public service as a higher calling. Adds Donahue: 'They take a lot of their pay in sunsets.'

"**Competition.** But more fundamentally, parks don't play to the strengths of the marketplace. The whole point of privatization is to tap competition; selling Yosemite to a commercial concern would merely convert a public monopoly into a private one. The park service certainly has its management failings — whole species have been threatened by park overcrowding, while buildings decay for lack of repair funds. But the market is unlikely to correct those mistakes, argues political scientist William Lowry, author of *The Capacity for Wonder*, a critical study of the park service. 'Markets work best when they can attach accurate prices to commodities,' explains Lowry. But accurate prices require that commodities have substitutes, so buyers and sellers can compare one with another. 'When you talk about the Grand Canyon,' says Lowry, 'there simply is no substitute.'***

---

*Author's Note: With superglue?
** " ": What an idea for a car-wash!
*** " ": Lowry has obviously never been to Arkansas' Hot Springs National Park.

"For an agency with a big public trust, the park service actually has privatized a vast array of services — from lodging to food service to trip outfitting. In fact, private concessionaires collected roughly $650 million in revenues from park patrons last year, while the park service itself collected just $76 million in fees — about 5 percent of its budget. In a nod to fiscal pressures in Washington, Kennedy has asked Congress for the power to raise park entrance fees — some of which haven't gone up since 1916 — by $32 million. Kennedy also wants to introduce more competition into the bidding process for park concessions, a step that could raise additional franchise revenues.

"Even so, Kennedy insists that Washington must draw a line between what properly belongs in the private sector and what should remain public. 'When consumers walk into Yellowstone,' he says, 'they expect something different from what they get in a theme park.' As Congress sifts through the privatization lists of Scott Klug and Al Gore, its biggest task may be to decide where the market can rule — and where it cannot."

****

There you have it. Don't be surprised if you walk into a voting booth someday to find a ballot that includes the following:

Should America's National Parks, Monuments, Seashores, Lakeshores, and Historic Sites be privatized?

Yes ☐   **No** ☐

You will be choosing between three options. You can maintain the status quo with a **No** vote. Rangers will continue working for low wages, partially compensated by clean air — except in units in the East and in California — and sunsets, and national parks will continue charging admission fees set in 1916.

Voting **Yes** opens the door to two scenarios.

PRIVATIZATION SCENARIO #1

Released from the shackles of administrative and political bureaucracy, rangers destroy backcountry roads built by their misguided overlords in years past. They allow wildfires to burn, as they did for thousands of years before people came along to save the wilderness from them. They dynamite dams, pausing to remember Edward Abbey.

The priorities of wildlife are put before those of visitors, allowing animals to actually flourish in their native ecosystems. Locally exterminated species are reintroduced. Americans once again thrill to the howls of wolves, the footprints of grizzly bears, the droppings that evidence the nocturnal foraging of black-footed ferrets.

And to reestablish the flow of genes that is as vital to biodiversity as modems are to computer hackers, rangers lay waste to vast swaths of civilized land separating the United States' wilderness reserves from a nation that is itself a wilderness reserve — Canada. Barbed wire is cut, highways and railroads torn up. For the first time in generations, large mammals can actually roam the West.

The wilderness reverts to wilderness, and concessions market this book, not as a statement of contemporary America, but as a souvenir of the days when environmental illiteracy was enhanced as *one nation under God* allowed its wilderness foundation to decay under an onslaught of bureaucracy and human population.

PRIVATIZATION SCENARIO #2

As you drive through a platinum arch bearing the words "Yellowstone Irrational Park, Inc." in enormous letters, "We Enhance the Wilderness" in smaller letters, a man in a bear costume rushes up and offers you a "Yellowstone Holiday" packet, advertising events, products, and services. Transportation fees vary. Will you tour the Park by monorail, car, van, mobile home, half-ton truck, motorcycle, bicycle, skateboard, rollerskates, helicopter, airplane, on horseback, or on foot? If you don't own a car, van, mobile home, half-ton truck, motorcycle, bicycle, skateboard, roller-skates, helicopter, airplane, or horse, you can rent one, along with lessons.

Once inside the amusement ecosystem you are dazzled by the diversity of attractions. You can watch world famous ice dancers at the Lewis & Clark Ice Palace. See the latest in fashions at the Teton Pavilion. *Shop 'till you drop* at the Yellowstone Mall.

Turn your kids loose on the myriad rides and attractions. The *Roller Toaster* is the *hottest* roller coaster around, giving riders a birds-eye view of Yellowstone's geothermal wonders. The *Wild Animal Stampede* is similar to a traditional pony-go-round, but the ponies are replaced by bison, elk, moose, and grizzly bears that grunt, bugle, and roar as they take riders on a cross-country circuit. Relive the Yellowstone fire of 1988 surrounded by the giant screens of the *Yellowstone OmniDome*. Cinematic flames are complemented by the faint whiff of smoke and a subtle rise in temperature as Smokey Bear sells popcorn.

Have lunch inside the giant *Beaver World Lodge*, which features the *Beaver Hall of Fame*, "a tribute to American thrift and industry." Here you can see relics of the fur trade; a collection of emblems and currency that depict beavers; life-size, animated black-bear sized prehistoric beavers known as *Castoroides*; and the fossil, corkscrew tunnels, or *diamonelix*, of a horned beaver ancestor that once inhabited the Great Plains.

Drop the kids off at the *Roosevelt Petting Zoo Nursery & Daycare Center* and relax for a couple hours. Or stop off at the *Yellowstone Home-Link Center*. Here you can access the latest in computer and communications technology to keep in touch with your home, business, friends and relatives. The staff can help you purchase a home or negotiate a business deal anywhere within the United States.

Then you can pick up the kids. Now might be a good time to sample some of Yellowstone's wilderness attractions. Myriad means of transportation can take you where the animals are, if your pockets are deep enough. If you have the time, you can participate in a buffalo hunt, help build a log cabin, or feed some bears.

"Wilderness enhancements" include Old Faithful, which spouts tributes to the 50 States. Floridians flock to the *Orange Show*, where waitresses offer iced orange juice to visitors enthralled by an orange gusher. Texans and Alaskans tremble with pride and excitement at the *Oil Boil*, when the Blue Angels streak overhead as a black gusher commemorates America's petroleum heritage. Revelers feast on barbecued steer and Eskimo Ice Cream, modified to suit Lower 48 palates. Choose from dozens of imported beers to wash it down with.

During the *Great Plains Extravaganza,* the reincarnation of Buffalo Bill's Wild West Show — cowboys and Indians on horseback whooping and shooting — circle Old Faithful as an orchestra plays the theme from Rogers and Hammerstein's *Oklahoma* and waiters dressed as characters from *The Wizard of Oz* hand out sunflower seeds.

But the grand finale occurs at night when Old Faithful erupts a gusher that alternates red, white, and blue, coordinated with an overhead fireworks display, as a symphony orchestra plays patriotic music.

Yellowstone Irrational Park, Inc. is about more than entertainment, however. Visitors not in a hurry to move on to the next Irrational Park, Inc. can attend the Rush Limbaugh School of Environmental Sciences. Learn why it's OK to cut down forests without fear of environmental effects. The school's motto is "We couldn't destroy Earth if we tried!"

Dreaming of a career working with natural resources? The Yellowstone Nature Academy offers courses in biology, geology, chemistry, theater and dance, business management, and commercial forest management. You may even get a job as a Nature Technician within the Irrational Park, Inc. empire. Of course, graduates ordinarily start at the bottom, which may mean managing lights during nocturnal productions, painting animal faces on children, or guiding visitors through the *Beaver Hall of Fame*.

But the benefits are unbeatable, including free shuttles to *real* semi-wilderness areas not too far from Yellowstone. The biggest benefit of all may be the security of belonging to a stable business enterprise coupled with the knowledge that upward mobility is guaranteed to anyone who works hard and dares to dream. And the franchise is branching into wilderness areas around the globe — Africa's Great Rift Valley, the Amazon, the Himalayas, Antarctica!

Why merely visit an Irrational Park, when you can become a part of the enterprise and share in the profits? Perhaps privatization of America's wonderlands isn't such a bad thing after all!

Cervid Metamorphosis

With New Discoveries Relating to "Prehistoric Relapse" and its Application to the Conservation of the Northern Great Plains Jack-a-lope, *Animalculus imitatans dakotah*

Dr. Heimlich Maneuvére, PhD[2]

Metamorphosis — literally, "changing" — is a phenomenon found in invertebrates, amphibians, and some fishes. Among warmblooded animals, metamorphosis is known to occur only among members of the family Cervidae, collectively known as cervids, or deer.

Because cervid metamorphosis is complex and involves so many species, there is much confusion outside the biological community concerning the origins of North America's native cervids. Rangers in America's wilderness preserves are frequently asked when the deer turn into elk, the elk into moose, etc. This brief account presents an overview of the phenomenon. It is hoped that rangers and other environmental educators can use it in educating the public about the origins of our "deerest" wildlife.

****

North America is inhabited by five native cervids — the moose (*Alces alces*), elk (*Cervus elaphus*), caribou (*Rangifer tarandus*), white-tailed deer (*Odocoileus virginianus*), and mule deer (*Odocoileus hemionus*) — and one pseudo-cervid, the jack-a-lope (*Animalculus imitatans*). Coincidentally, the life cycles of all six species are precariously linked to one of North America's most endangered ecosystems — that portion of the Northern Great Plains lying between the Rocky Mountains in Wyoming and the Missouri River in South Dakota, bordered to the north and south by the Badlands of North Dakota and South Dakota. The approximate center of this ecosystem is Belle Fourche, South Dakota, near the geographic center of North America.

In autumn, jack-a-lopes begin to congregate on buttes rising above the grasslands in preparation for a great migrational flight to their metamorphosing grounds. Triggered by some yet unknown environmental, hormonal, or behavioral stimulus, they leap en masse into the air on the darkest night of the month and begin flying northwest towards the Canadian Rockies. Upon reaching the mountains, they divide into smaller bands which search for glacial cirques on southern slopes. There they weave cocoons in which they will metamorphose — very slowly in winter, but more rapidly in spring and summer, when the days grow longer.

Upon emerging — as white-tailed or mule deer, depending on which side of the continental divide they're on — they slide down avalanche chutes. Mule and white-tailed deer may produce progeny through live birth up to thirteen generations after hatching from a cocoon; the fourteenth generation is sterile. Therefore, the population must be replenished by jack-a-lopes approximately once a century.

When populations become particularly dense, hormonal changes cause deer to become restless, similar to a Rocky Mountain locust or northern lemmings, and they may develop into a slightly longer-legged migratory form. These "locust deer" ("lemming deer" to Canadians) begin wandering restlessly while eating voraciously.

The enhanced hormonal flow causes a return to a neotenous, or juvenile, condition while the increased dietary intake accelerates growth. Under such conditions, mule deer may metamorphose into elk, whitetails into moose.

Moose that reside in the northernmost taiga and tundra regions may in turn undergo *solar metamorphosis* to become caribou. The process begins when intense sunspot activity causes the *Aurora borealis* ("northern lights") to flare with exceptional brightness. Moose that are particularly light-sensitive may seek relief from the auroral flares by burrowing under snow on frozen rivers and entering a state of arrested metabolism which scientists once mistook for hibernation. As the rivers break up in spring, the frozen moose slowly float upstream until their icy chambers melt, exposing caribou.

The common belief that Old World cervids do not metamorphose has been challenged by evidence of similarities between the tissues of the extinct Irish elk (*Megaloceros*) and the jack-a-lope. Scientists postulate that vast flocks of jack-a-lopes once regularly exhausted precious cocoon space in the Canadian Rockies' glacial cirques. According to this theory, excess jack-a-lopes flew to Delaware, replenished their reserves by feasting on horseshoe crabs, and embarked on a trans-Atlantic flight to the British Isles. There are no glacial cirques in the British Isles comparable to those of the Canadian Rockies. But these wayward jack-a-lopes apparently found Ireland's peat bogs to their liking. Today, Ireland's peat bogs yield fossils of the so-called "Irish elk," which are more a product of South Dakota than Ireland, just as Idaho's *Famous Potatoes* really belong to Ireland.

Stories alleging that elk or caribou can transform into other cervids — or jack-a-lopes — are preposterous, with no basis whatsoever in science. With one solitary exception, reverse metamorphosis simply does not occur in Nature. And of course, neither elk nor moose give birth to jack-a-lopes, nor do any New World mammals lay eggs. So where do jack-a-lopes come from?

For generations, this ranked with the origins of Spam and dry ice as one of science's greatest mysteries. Only in recent years was it solved, and then only through the collaboration of zoologists, paleontologists, meteorologists, and historians from South Dakota State University (Brookings), The University of Calgary (Alberta), the University of Alaska at Fairbanks, and the Chinese Academy of Sciences (Beijing). Following is the dramatic saga which unfolded before scientists' eyes.

Some thirteen million years ago during the Miocene Epoch, cervids (deer) and lagomorphs (rabbits and hares) shared a common, antlered ancestor that inhabited what is now China. This proto-jack-a-lope (*Bunny sinensis*) preyed primarily on primitive pheasants that shared its tropical forest home. Over a period of millions of years, it evolved elongated hind legs that enabled it to leap high into the air and, later, small wings that enabled it to continue aerial pursuit of its prey. Later still, it developed collapsible antlers and a pheasant-like tail that helped it stalk its unsuspecting prey. It had become a jack-a-lope.

During the Pleistocene, or "Ice Age," the jack-a-lope and the horse became extinct in Asia and North America, respectively. However, each species had crossed the Bering Land Bridge into the other's native continent. (Biogeographers term such a phenomenon a *faunal bypass*.) The evolutionary paths of the two expatriate species differed dramatically. Maintaining their niche as grasslands herbivores, horses were not under great evolutionary pressure to change; the zebra's stripes are only skin deep, so to speak. Diet compelled the jack-a-lope, on the other hand, to undergo drastic morphological, physiological, and behavioral changes.

As pheasants are not native to North America, the New World jack-a-lope adapted to a diet of rodents. With energy-draining extremities a maladaptation in the Far North, the jack-a-lope gradually lost its wings and tail feathers, though it kept its antlers for digging through snow and ice in search of rodents, mating displays, and defense against predators. Its hind legs were also markedly reduced in size, and it developed a loping gait. Scientists call this species, whose antlers and teeth are commonly found in gravel bars along Alaskan rivers, *Bunny beringiana*.

Competition with other predators — such as foxes, lynxes, and wolverines — and a changing climate further refined *Bunny beringiana*'s dietary adaptations. As the antlers became reduced in size, it relied more on speed for eluding predators, and its hind legs reverted to their primordial form. This was the "French hare" (*Bunny yukonnais*), so-called because its fossils were first discovered by French-Canadian voyageurs in the Yukon. The French hare radiated throughout North America, evolving into hares and rabbits.

Just as some people have vestigial tails, so does the white-tailed jackrabbit (*Lepus townsendii*) carry recessive genes for antlers. Scientists think that some unidentified mineral or minerals in Northern Great Plains soils — perhaps stirred up by pawing bison — formerly stimulated hormones, which in turn caused antlers to erupt. These antlered jackrabbits then proceeded to metamorphose into full-fledged jack-a-lopes. When white settlers invaded the Great Plains, exterminating bison and converting the land to agriculture, the phenomenon apparently ceased — only to reappear in the greatest scientific coincidence of the 20th century.

That there is apparently a thirteen-year time lag between initial hormonal stimulation and the actual eruption of jack-a-lope antlers was first noticed by historians: Jack-a-lope populations appeared to be particularly high thirteen years after the filming of a bison stampede in South Dakota for the movie *How the West Was Won*.

Jack-a-lope researchers were struck by the fact that the animal had first reappeared approximately thirteen years after the Chinese ring-necked pheasant (*Phasianus colchicus*) was first introduced to South Dakota in notable numbers in 1914.* What possible connection could there be between bison and pheasants?

The missing piece to the puzzle was discovered just a few years later when Chinese poachers in pursuit of a giant panda stumbled upon the exquisitely-preserved remains of a jack-a-lope family. Preserved along with them were feathers that were unmistakably pheasant in origin. With more fieldwork and laboratory analysis, the jack-a-lope's enigmatic evolutionary and natural history came to light.

Endocrinologists put the final piece of the puzzle in place, revealing what had caused jack-a-lope to reappear on the Dakota plains: The sight of ringnecks — or even the sound of one crowing — stimulates hormones that induce the growth of antlers on jackrabbits.

The stress imposed on their bodies by the rapid antler growth induces these "spike hares" to seek a high-protein diet. Additional recessive genes come into play, causing the animals to revert to their primordial role as pheasant hunters.

A steady diet of pheasants does more than promote antler growth, however. In a science fantasy that transcends the movie *Jurassic Park*, it also stimulates still more recessive genes to express themselves, and the animal grows wings and tail feathers. What was once a jackrabbit has retraced its evolutionary history through reverse metamorphosis to become a prehistoric jack-a-lope.

Although the jack-a-lope is one of the world's natural wonders, it is also a serious threat to the nation's pheasant-hunting capital, preying on both pheasants and cereal grains and impacting tourism. Jack-a-lopes have been known to dart into Wall Drug and freeze, posing as mounted specimens. A second jack-a-lope screams and leaps about outside, causing diners to look out the window. The "frozen" jack-a-lope then comes to life and grabs food off the nearest table. Wall Drug personnel note that jack-a-lopes display a preference for buffalo burgers.

---

*George Washington was the first American to import Chinese ring-necked pheasants. This fact doubtless inspired rumors that jack-a-lopes are especially common around Mt. Rushmore, which depicts George Washington's likeness. These rumors are, of course, nonsense. In fact, personnel at Mt. Rushmore National Memorial state that jack-a-lopes are practically unknown near Mt. Rushmore, as they are in the Black Hills in general. They also emphasize that there are no Roosevelt elk, Lincoln moles, or Jefferson ground sloths in the Black Hills.

Millions of years ago, odd-toed mammals, or perissodactyls, were the dominant herbivores. These include rhinoceroses, tapirs, and horses, which are now represented primarily by several endangered species. The dominant herbivores today are even-toed mammals, or artiodactyls. These animals have in turn branched into pigs and peccaries, camels, bovids (horned mammals), and cervids (deer). Fossils of an animal with long canines suggest a common ancestor of both the proto-jack-a-lope and the diminutive, primitive muntjacs, or barking deer, and musk deer which still inhabit Asia's tropical forests. Why did these canines evolve into tusks in the case of herbivorous deer, yet disappear in the omnivorous jack-a-lope? Deer tusks are defensive, rather than dietary, adaptations. Preying primarily on small animals — particularly pheasants — the jack-a-lope had no need for tusks, which reached their pinnacle among terrestrial carnivores among the saber-toothed cats and catlike marsupials. The illustrations of the muntjac and skull above appeared in the *Proceedings of the Zoological Society of London* in 1874. In both muntjacs and musk deer, the canines develop into tusks only in males.

Finally, jack-a-lopes commonly cause power outages during the rutting season. Their antlers become entangled in power lines when the animals make their spectacular courtship leaps. It is postulated that their apparent attraction to sources of electricity is evidence of a sensitivity to Earth's magnetic field.

The jack-a-lope's ability to both run and fly, its great intelligence, and its capacity to literally "breed like a rabbit" make it even more difficult to eliminate than the coyote. The State of South Dakota offers bounties on jack-a-lopes. A few jack-a-lopes — generally young males or senile individuals of either gender — have been captured by hunters imitating pheasants, or using pheasant decoys. Jack-a-lopes are generally far too clever to be duped by these methods, however. The South Dakota Department of Game, Fish, and Parks has experimented with helicopters carrying marksmen. While effective, this method is also prohibitively expensive.

The Department encourages ranchers and farmers to cooperate in forming "jack-a-lope posses" which pursue jack-a-lopes on horseback, unleashing falcons on their prey when they flush. Besides promoting togetherness and friendship in a state already known for its hospitality, the generous bounties collected by such posses help diversify South Dakota's economy. Many of South Dakota's grain silos, community water towers, and outdoor movie screens were paid for with jack-a-lope bounties. The book *(IR)Rational Parks* was partially funded by a jack-a-lope grant.

Jack-a-lope bounties may only be collected by native-born South Dakotans, though nonresidents who take up residence in South Dakota and are not behind on their child support or student loan payments may apply for a provisional permit after demonstrating their skills in horsemanship and falconry.

Just before jack-a-lopes depart on their metamorphic flights, their meat takes on a flavor remarkably similar to red snapper. But jack-a-lope meat is generally described as tasting like a cross between sage grouse and its primary diet — sage. South Dakotans like to marinate premigratory jack-a-lopes — commonly called "sage jack" — in a mixture of beer and tomato juice spiced with copious amounts of dill. The mixture is set out in the hot sun until all the liquids have evaporated. The animal is then barbecued after being drenched with any number of sauces. Various families, jack-a-lope posses, and counties each have their favorite — and generally secret — recipes.

There has been talk of establishing a barbecued jack-a-lope food chain. However, no one has yet been able to raise large populations of jack-a-lopes in captivity. Such meat products as "West Coast Jack-A-Lope," "Great Lakes Jack-A-Lope," "Texarkana Jack-A-Lope," etc., are generally derived from other animals. The State of South Dakota currently has lawsuits pending against vendors in forty-five states. (Alaskans are allowed to market meat products as "Jack-a-lope" under a special trans-Canadian treaty.)

While jack-a-lope fur is unremarkable, the unique combination of fur and feathers make jack-a-lope pelts a luxury item. However, it is illegal to sell jack-a-lope pelts, as jack-a-lopes are protected by migratory bird treaties. (Report attempted sales of jack-a-lope "furthers!" Call the National Audubon Society's Jack-a-lope Hotline, 1 (800) JAK-LOPE.)

Though rivaled in intelligence only by primates and marine mammals, jack-a-lopes do not make good pets or work animals. Like Great Plains residents, they are simply too independent. Moreover, they seemingly cannot be cured from attacking poultry and stampeding through fields of corn or wheat, apparently to satisfy their predatory urges. They also wreak havoc on antennas and satellite dishes.

There is great fear in China that jack-a-lopes may be reintroduced into their endangered tropical forests, where they would prey on even more endangered pheasants. Authorities in South Dakota and China are cooperating in developing strategies for keeping this unique symbol of prehistoric China contained in the northern Great Plains. Although they have explored the most technologically advanced strategies scientists have devised, the most effective method discovered to date is, appropriately, one of the most primitive: Jack-a-lope hounds patrol all North American airports serving China.

Do you have a favorite jack-a-lope recipe you would like to share? If so, send it to Jack-a-lope Recipes, Geobopological Survey, PO Box 95465, Seattle, WA 98145.

PREFACE

Traditionally, the Preface appears before a book's Introduction. But America wasn't built by people who bowed to tradition. Placing the Preface in the Appendix is my way of flouting my independence.

Typically dull, prefaces are frequently ignored by readers anyway. This Preface is duller than most. Why turn off potential customers with a dull beginning when I can hide it in the back of the book?

If I had simply deleted the Preface, I might have been able to shave twenty cents off the book's price. For readers who want their twenty cents' worth, here is your Preface.

****

During the last week of January, 1995, I was reminiscing about some of the humorous tourist questions I had heard fellow rangers laughing about when I worked for the National Park Service at Grand Teton National Park, Wyoming some ten years earlier. It struck me that a compilation of similar questions and anecdotes from the nation's national parks and monuments might be entertaining.

I wrote to the more than 350 units administered by the National Park Service (NPS), a few allied agencies, and numerous concessions. Responses were divided between admonitions that my project was inappropriate (no anecdotes enclosed), congratulations on such an exciting idea and encouragement (with or without enclosed anecdotes), and official literature (brochures, etc.) with no comments whatsoever.

I had *Desert Solitaire* on my mind from the beginning. Written by the late Edward Abbey, a former Park Ranger, this classic has always ranked with Aldo Leopold's *Sand County Almanac* as one of my environmental bibles. Abbey had a lot to say about our vanishing wilderness, government bureaucracy, and cultural decay — the decay of civilization might be a better way to put it. He also had a keen sense of humor. His book included a number of amusing quips and conversations with tourists.

I adopted Abbey's book and philosophy — which is similar to mine anyway — as something of a guide. I don't mean to imply that Abbey would have endorsed my book, though I suspect he would have. (I never met or corresponded with Edward Abbey.)

Imagine, if you will, a fusion of *Desert Solitaire* and the magazine *National Lampoon*. (This may be difficult for readers who have read neither.) As preposterous as it sounds, that's sort of how I envision my book.

I wrote this book in the belief — or hope — that most readers can differentiate between a humorous put-down and a blatant insult and secure enough to endure exposure of certain individual and cultural foibles. I also advised correspondents that I would not print their names without permission. (Any anonymous contributors who wish to be credited in revisions or in a projected sequel are invited to contact me.)

This book is not meant to create the impression that rangers have a cynical attitude towards visitors. On the contrary, most National Park Service and USDA Forest Service personnel are extremely professional. They don't need to be advised by administrators to be courteous and understanding any more than teachers need administrators to admonish them to care about kids. During the summer I worked at Grand Teton National Park, I never witnessed any of my colleagues treating visitors with rudeness or contempt.

As a naturally inquisitive person and a writer, I've asked countless questions, many of them exceedingly trivial or off-the-wall. I've been laughed at and insulted many times, but I keep right on asking. It's my observation that people who laugh at people who ask unusual questions are frequently lacking in mental prowess themselves.

Nevertheless, I'm extremely interested in how, if at all, this book affects National Park Service/Forest Service personnel and the visitors they interact with. I've tried to ensure that all the material I present as fact is indeed factual, while any nonsense I include is (hopefully) nonsensical. (No attempt has been made to verify the authenticity of any anecdotes or visitors' questions that were sent to me, however.)

Writing this book was like writing a love letter. The initial inspiration struck me like a thunderbolt. From that moment on, I was overflowing with complex emotions and ideas that were very difficult to transfer to paper. I'm eager for readers to tell me what I've created!

Some brief comments on the questions, quips, and anecdotes themselves are in order. The materials I received varied from photocopies of logbooks to handwritten or typed letters. Some of the logbooks, in particular, were very inconsistent in format, spelling, abbreviations, etc. Accordingly, I've taken some liberties in reproducing certain materials, sometimes correcting spelling or grammar, adding or deleting quotations, etc. The materials I received reflect a breadth of humor. And not all the questions, quips, and observations are humorous. Some are witty, others philosophical, and still others simply educational. Of course, you're already aware of all this because you've already read the book!

****

Do my comments on bureaucracies suggest a personal animosity towards the National Park Service's bureaucracy? No.

As Edward Abbey noted, the National Park Service is subject to powerful forces, as are the reserves it is sworn to protect. I worked for the organization too briefly to really become well acquainted with it. I certainly never had any unpleasant experiences with the few National Park Service administrators I met, who seemed to be pretty decent people.

Abbey judged the National Park Service as better than most federal bureaucracies, giving most of the credit to the rank and file — the rangers in the field. Keep in mind that many National Park Service administrators come from such roots and never lose sight of the awesome mission with which they are both charged and privileged.

THE WEST

The United States is bordered on the north by its

WASHINGTON

● Seattle
Mt. Rainier NP
Mt. St. Helens
Volcanic NM

Missouri

MONTANA

Little Bighorn
Battlefield NM

OREGON

IDAHO

Yellowstone NP

Crater Lake NP
(Caution: The crater
is full of water.)

Craters of
the Moon
NM

Grand Teton NP

Devils
Tower
NM

Hagerman
Fossil Beds NM

WYOMING

CALIFORNIA

NEVADA

With its motto,
"Battle Born," Nevada
might be considered
one big monument
to the Civil War.

Golden
Spike NHS

Rocky Mt.
NP COLORADO

Muir
Woods NM

Florissant
Fossil Beds NM

UTAH

Yosemite NP

Great Sand
Dunes NM

Bent's Old
Fort NHS

Death Valley NM

Mesa Verde NP

Santa Monica
Mts. NRA

Grand Canyon NP

Capulin Volcano NM

ARIZONA

NEW MEXICO

Channel
Islands NP
(Caution: These
islands are sur-
rounded by water.)

Petrified
Forest NP

(USS *Arizona*
Memorial)

(Petrified Forest NP,
Argentina)

Carlsbad
Caverns NP

MAP OF THE GREAT
AMERICAN WILDERNESS

This map is based on material the author received in response to his queries for humorous visitors' questions from units administered by the National Park Service. Units that do not provoke such questions are presumably ordinary, dull, and boring and therefore qualify as neither natural nor cultural wilderness areas. This map omits Kansas, Oklahoma, the Midwest, and a few states in the South. Despite its great size, spirit, and fabulous flag, Texas, which made no contributions, is also omitted. Space precludes the depiction of Alaska, Hawaii, and the moon.

THE DAKOTAS

NEWFOUNDLAND, NORWAY

largest wilderness preserve, CANADA.

1) Belle Fourche (GEOGRAPHIC CENTER OF THE U.S.)
2) Mt. Rushmore Nat. Memorial
3) Hot Springs (home of The Mammoth Site)
4) Badlands NP
5) Wall (& WALL DRUG)
6) Kadoka (Outhouse Races!) 7) Pierre
8) Winner
9) Chamberlain
10) Mitchell

NORTH DAKOTA

Missouri River

Theodore Roosevelt NP

SOUTH DAKOTA

Chimney Rock NHS
Scotts Bluff NM

NEBRASKA

Mt. Katahdin

MAINE

VT
NH
Cape Cod NS

Saratoga NHS

NEW YORK
Martin Van Buren NHS

MASS.

PENNSYLVANIA

Valley Forge NHP
Gettysburg NMP

Haddonfield, NEW JERSEY

Harpers Ferry NHP

Washington, D.C. (& Wash. Monument)

Fredericksburg and Spotsylvania County Battlefields Memorial NMP

New River Gorge National River

WEST VA

VIRGINIA

KENTUCKY

Mammoth Cave NP

Booker T. Washington NM

Great Smoky Mts. NP

NORTH CAROLINA

THE EAST

TENNESSEE

regrettable omissions:

Indiana Dunes NL is in Indiana, by the Great lakes

(continued below)

Chickamauga and Chattanooga NMP

SOUTH CAROLINA

Congaree Swamp NM

GEORGIA

Gulf Islands NP
St. Vincent Island NWR

FLORIDA

Jefferson Expansion Nat. Memorial is in St. Louis, Missouri, on the Missouri River

Pea Ridge NMP is in Arkansas

LEGEND:

- Generic National Parks
- Underground Nat. Parks
- Other Units Administered by the Nat. Park Service
- Units administered by other agencies
- ☺ Capital Cities
- ● Other Communities
- ▲ Mountain
- Geographic Center of the U.S.

SCALE: Much smaller than the real United States

INTERACTIVE PAGES

These two pages are symbolic of your personality. If they remain blank, chances are *you're* a blank. These pages are provided for your convenience in recording humorous utterances or anecdotes, personal thoughts or experiences, poetry, etc. You might want to paste pictures on these pages or press leaves between them.

If you're alarmed at the steady loss of wilderness and biodiversity, on the other hand, you may want to leave these pages blank. Mail a copy of this book to your representatives in Washington, D.C. and advise them that the blank pages symbolize the support they can expect from you if they don't do something to reverse the tide.

232

INDEX

Announcing a Sequel

Some readers may think the bear on the cover is Smokey Bear. It is not. I requested permission to depict Smokey, but my request was denied. Thank God.

Smokey Bear is not a suitable ambassador for this series, in which bears play a prominent role. For although Smokey is typically portrayed as a guardian of the wilderness, he isn't. My bear is.

Bears, the decline of Western civilization through the loss of wilderness and biodiversity, and America's public education wilderness are among the themes I will tentatively focus on in the sequel. But there won't be a sequel unless you pitch in. For this book is but the beginning of a series which is a cooperative project. I need input from United States citizens and welcome input from residents of other nations as well.

Do you have an item you'd like to share? It can be a question, quip, anecdote, or anything that is humorous, unusual, provocative. The American wilderness, its wild residents, and civilized guardians and visitors are but the nucleus of this series.

Your contribution may relate to a visitor, ranger, wildlife biologist, geologist or miner, environmentalists, anti-environmentalists, bureaucrats and politicians. Indeed, I would like to broaden my foundation and am requesting material relating to the following:

1) **State Parks**

2) **Foreign Wilderness or Nature Preserves**

3) **Cultural Tourism** — Have you had an amusing or unusual experience while visiting one of the world's great cities, an archaeological dig, an art museum, fashion show, or a kibbutz?

4) **Zoological Parks and Aquariums** — What are some amusing questions you've heard visitors ask? What amusing or unusual experiences have zookeepers had while working with animals?

5) **Museums and Scientists** — What weird questions have you been asked? What have been some of your weirdest projects, discoveries, or accomplishments?

6) **Chambers of Commerce, Historical Societies, Libraries** — What offbeat questions have you been asked?

7) **Litigation and the American Wilderness** — I need true stories about people who have sued because they got hurt when they stuck their foot in hot lava, were attacked by an animal they tried to feed, or got hit in the head by a rock or chunk of ice. How about stranded mountain climbers who expect to be rescued at taxpayers' expense? How is our legal system impacting the National Park Service, allied agencies, and visitors?

8) **Education** — Attention public school teachers (especially those who work as rangers during summers): As a teacher, I will have lots to say about public education in America.

9) **Bureaucracy** — Do you have any funny or unbelievable stories that relate to this cultural phenomenon?

10) **Fire** — How is the federal bureaucracy's crusade against forest fires similar to its efforts in the arena of public education? I need information on firefighting politics in presenting this revelation.

11) **Bears!**

12) I'm always in the market for the standard verbal bloopers heard in America's wilderness preserves, concessions, and urban wilderness.

When submitting material, try to include such background information as location, date, etc. If submitting an article from a newspaper or magazine, please note what issue and date it appeared in. Humorous or unusual pictures are welcome.

Anonymity is guaranteed; names of contributors will be featured only if specifically requested. Please don't send material anonymously, however. I may need to contact you for details or to request legal permission to reprint your contribution.

****

If you don't have any information to share, you can still get your name on a mailing list for notification when the sequel is finished. Please address related correspondence to one of the following:

Contributions
Geobopological Survey
PO Box 95465
Seattle, WA 98145-2465

Sequel Mailing List
Geobopological Survey
PO Box 95465
Seattle, WA 98145-2465

Remember, this is *our* sequel.

Order Form

(IR)Rational Parks makes a great gift. Interpreters and naturalists, consult *(IR)Rational Parks* for insights into dealing with tricky visitors' questions. Concessions and guide companies — present copies to your employees and clients at the end of their outdoor adventure for a memento they'll never forget! Visitors — enjoy *(IR)Rational Parks* on rainy days or while waiting in those long lines at Yellowstone, Yosemite, and other American wonderlands. Foreign visitors — ask rangers to interpret this book into your native tongue.

To order a copy of *(IR)Rational Parks*, send a check made out to "Geobop" for $15.95 ($13.95 + $2.00 shipping) to Geobopological Survey, PO Box 95465-B, Seattle, WA 98145-2465. USA. (206) 527-1690 Add $1.00 shipping for each additional book ordered. Residents of Washington (State, not D.C.) — add 8.2% for sales tax.

Name:_____

Company/Organization/Agency:_____

Address:_____

City:_____ State:_____ Zip:_____-_____

Favorite Bear:_____